Every journey requires a compass. Through *Life's Concerto*, Terri Goslin-Jones lays out one such compass, that of poetry and expressive arts. This work can serve as a guidebook to those traveling alone or with companions; it depends entirely on the depth of excavation one is willing to do within themselves. Expressing oneself through poetry is a necessity on this journey, while the expressive arts serve as stepping stones down the path of the pilgrimage within. This book is a beautiful companion to the traveler who has just taken their first steps and to the one who is already well on their journey.

Bahareh Amidi, PhD, Poet, Educator, Social Activist

Terri Goslin-Jones creatively and wholeheartedly shares a journey of wholeness through poetry and expressive arts. After reading *Life's Concerto,* I am excited to recommend this book to those who are searching for poetic inspiration about life and in-depth knowledge via soulful words. As an expressive arts therapist, I see possibilities of wisdom emerging to breathe, play, imagine, create, listen, improvise, understand, heal, and be transformed from poetry.

Fiona Chang-Foo, PhD, REAT, RSW, Certified Supervisor, Founding President, Expressive Arts Therapy Association of Hong Kong, Faculty, Person-Centered Expressive Arts

Psyche is made conscious only when it inhabits an image, be it in the body, in one's patterns, or in dreams. Terri Goslin-Jones' *Life's Concerto* is a summons and a guide to activate the psyche, see what images arise, and to enlarge conscious life by including the energies each image brings. In this way, one begins to integrate those aspects of one's soul otherwise denied, buried, split off. As a result, one grows less at odds with oneself.

James Hollis, PhD, Jungian analyst in Washington, DC and Author

Terri Goslin-Jones and her unique *Concerto* make an inspiring new contribution to the 'universal story' of how art heals everywhere, now and in the past. The sharing of her poems, together with rich visual imagery, revives the tradition of illuminated manuscripts, crystallized by the Monastic Mother series, inviting the creation of sacred places for artistic expression in each of us.

Shaun McNiff, PhD, author of *Trust the Process: An Artist's Guide to Letting Go, Art as Medicine, Art Heals, Imagination in Action: Secrets for Unleashing Creative Expression*, and other books

Let me first share on a personal level my respect for Terri Goslin-Jones' deep commitment to staying faithful to the creative journey and facing all its facets with humble dignity and creative and poetic practice. And—I love the artwork! It is my pleasure to quote the author of *Life's Concerto* herself:

> 'I do not want to be a crooked elder,
> who cannot look people in the eye. …
> Why can't I –
> adjust and accept,
> micro breakdowns
> and shifts inside my body? …
> Why wait for heaven, when the
> Garden of Eden
> resides in your backyard? …
> Here am I …
> adventure is essential,
> to stay alert and alive. …'

> Professor Margo Fuchs Knill, PhD, Founding Dean, Core Faculty, Division Arts, Health and Society, European Graduate School

The dawn of humanity saw the birth of the expressive arts as early humans drew, painted, danced, and chanted to enhance their connections with each other, with nature and the cosmos. Terri Goslin-Jones is a contemporary player in this tradition, using poetry and other arts to express her feelings and to share her wisdom with her fortunate readers and students. *Life's Concerto* is one of those rare books that will continue to inspire and instruct long after it is read.

> Stanley Krippner, PhD, Psychologist, Researcher, Author, and Professor at California Institute of Integral Studies

Reading Terri Goslin-Jones book awakens a deep and transformative yearning for wholeness—through nature, through poetry, through creative expression. Her new book, *Life's Concerto*, is a celebration of life and *Kairos*, life-time, awakening time. Don't miss it.

> Donald Moss, PhD, Professor and Dean, College of Integrative Medicine and Health Sciences, Saybrook University

WELCOME to a mystical and multisensory experience, a beautiful journey of holistic discovery, intertwined poetry, photography, and visual art. *Life's Concerto* gives to each of us, the visionary reader (that is, to you and me, with a vast inner world unfolding in turn), an openness, adventure, and entanglement with life and one another. There is a seeking beyond illusions of fixed self to a fluid interdependence, a renewed sense of self-in-world, in a sea of change and mystery unseen, in vastness unmeasured, with a willingness to see anew and to know the self, world, and all beings in fresh ways. The book builds and deepens—and it never ends. Nor should it. Plus, in some ways, as the poet says, we remain part of this—always. Our truest mission is love. Do not miss this beautiful book.

Ruth Richards, MD, PhD, Professor Emerita,
Saybrook University, Creativity Studies & Consciousness,
Spirituality, and Integrative Health. Author of *Everyday Creativity and the Healthy Mind: Dynamic New Paths for Self and Society*
(Silver Nautilus Award)

Life's Concerto bids us enter two worlds at once—the world of reader and the world of co-creator. As Terri Goslin-Jones writes, "We travel together as part of a universal field." This book is radiant proof that such collaborative journeying is possible. Through paintings, photographs, and poems—plus a host of resources including ideas to leap into your own creative practice—she offers us both inspiration and generous invitation. It's a cocoon of a book. "Unbolt your inner threshold," she encourages. "Dear One, you are safe to create."

Rosemerry Wahtola Trommer, MA, author of *The Unfolding*
and host of *The Poetic Path* on the Ritual App

At a time when our world seems tumultuous and troubling, the book *Life's Concerto*, written by Terri Goslin-Jones, PhD, provides readers both an anchor and a salve that soothes. Terri's book of heart-stopping poetry offers both an internal swim to soulful depths and a glorious creative study of our external world—both essential in grasping the lessons of life. As Terri states in her book, "Writing a poem is a way to cross over into an internal dwelling space and find puzzle pieces." Her new book provides both exercises to join this creative process for one's own growth, and poetic expressions of the heart and spirit to inspire and rise above the challenges we face.

Anin Utigaard, MFT, REAT, IEATA Co-Founder

Life's Concerto: Wholeness through Poetry and Expressive Arts

By Terri Goslin-Jones

Colorado Springs, CO
www.universityprofessorspress.com

Copyright © 2025 Terri Goslin-Jones
Life's Concerto: Wholeness through Poetry and Expressive Arts
By Terri Goslin-Jones

All rights reserved. No portion of this book may be reproduced by any process or technique without the express written consent of the publishers.

ISBN (Color Photo Version):   978-1-955737-62-3
ISBN (Black & White Photo Version): 978-1-955737-63-0
ISBN (Ebook):   978-1-955737-64-7

University Professors Press
Colorado Springs, CO
www.universityprofessorspress.com

All images, photographs, and artwork by Terri Goslin-Jones.

Cover Image by Terri Goslin-Jones
Cover Design adapted by Laura Ross

Table of Contents

Gratitude	i
Foreword by John Fox	iii
Introduction	1
Section I	9
What Sides of Myself Need to Be Heard?	
1) Sleep to Wake	9
2) What Sides of Myself Need to be Heard?	12
3) Close In	13
4) Inner Neighborhood	14
5) Creative Quest	16
6) Longing is the Music of my Soul	18
7) Letter from My Magical, Mystical Guide	19
Section II	21
Tidal Waves	
1) Daybreak at Seabrook	23
2) Little Tree from the Sea	24
3) Mother Sea Turtle	25
4) Poetic Promise	27
5) Ocean Tides Chant	28
6) Tidal Waves	29
7) Sacred Depth	31
8) Whispering Wind	32
9) Transcendent Tides	34
Section III	37
Time to Turn: Ancient Monastery	
1) Time to Turn	39
2) Tree of Life Hermitage	41
3) Ancient Monastery	43
4) Surrender	44
5) Ash Mystery	45
6) Shadow Speaks	46
7) Crossing Over	47
8) Contemplation: My Mom's Death	49

Section IV 53
The Cracked Hallelujah
1) Time Traveler 55
2) Dream Mirror 56
3) Where Did He Go? 59
4) Reverse Birthing 60
5) Family Roots 62
6) Grief's Ground Takes Root 64
7) Explore the Tornado's Roar 67
8) Velvet Cocoon 69
9) The Wild One 70
10) Reclaim the Stranger Within 75

Section V 79
Monastic Mother
1) Monastic Mother (Poem collage 2017–2021) 81
2) Gathering Her Wits 83
3) This Too Shall Pass 84
4) A Mother's Vow 86
5) Life's Concerto 89
6) Cloud Calligraphy 92
7) Thanksgiving Table 94
8) NorthStar Cherry Season 96
9) Magnolia Family Tree 98

Section VI 99
Gardener of the Soul
1) Our TerryHill Lane Garden 101
2) Gardener of the Soul 104
3) Owl Medicine 105
4) Cicadas Line Dance 106
5) Nature's Secret Messages 107
6) Life on the Web 108
7) Tree Spirit Summons 109
8) Born from the Heavens 111
9) Dawn's Chorus 112

Section VII
Miracles at Play   115
- 1) Stunned with Grace   117
- 2) Silence is the Portal to My Soul   118
- 3) Mississippi River's Sunrise Surprise   119
- 4) Miracles at Play   120
- 5) Universal Circle   122
- 6) My Moon's Embrace   124
- 7) Lost in Medical Measures   125
- 8) Dear Body   127
- 9) Here Am I   129
- 10) Free Solo   130

Letter to Reader   131
Addendum A: Writing Invitations   133
Addendum B: Poetry Resources   139
About the Author   145

Gratitude

"I must be a mermaid. I have no fear of depths
and a great fear of shallow living."
— Anais Nin

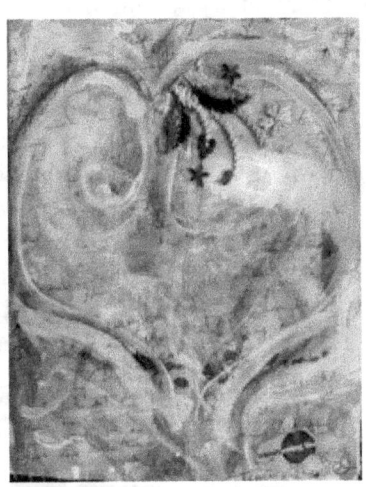

Poetry, artmaking, and photography are numinous gifts that help me excavate and express encounters with my inner world. It is essential to be accompanied by loving partners during these creative expeditions.

I want to express my heartfelt gratitude to Janet Childs, Cyra Dumitru, and John Fox for your poetic medicine and compassionate mentorship during our Institute of Poetic Medicine training program.

Thank you to our IPM cohort of poets: Analicia, Barbara, E.D., Jim, Lisha, Marcie, Marshall, Trina, Witek, and my sister sojourner/co-facilitator, Susan. It has been special to grow together, to expand our voices, and to share poetic medicine with our communities. Our IPM community "left footprints on my heart."

With loving appreciation to my beloved husband, Bob. We grew up together. You listened to every dream and every poem I wrote during our precious garden walks through life. When I get lost underground or lost in space, you help me find my way home. Eternal love to our sons Bobby and Matt. Being a parent is a sacred path. It is an honor and joy to be your mom. My life and my heart are more expansive because of you.

With love to my precious Creative Spirit Circle sisters, Ginger, Holly, Kim, Pam, and Nancy, for our shared community and commitment to *Weaving Ourselves Whole* as we walk each other home in this inspiring final quartile of life.

Gratitude and love to my lifelong sisterhood community for encouraging each other to persevere and flourish through life's challenges and to celebrate our joys: Agnes, Barb, Beth, Connie, Cyra, Darlene, Debbie, Deb, Janet, Maria, Mary, Mona, Pati, Susan, Tamara, and Vicki.

I value my Saybrook University community for sharing my journey and explorations of conscious transformation, and especially my cherished mentors Steve Pritzker, PhD., Ruth Richards, MD, PhD, and Natalie Rogers, PhD.

I thank University Professors Press and Louis Hoffman, PhD, for your commitment to publish poetry that heals. With endless gratitude to Cyra Dumitru, my poetry mentor, colleague, and dear friend who helped me unearth and share my poetic voice.

I am grateful to my ancestors for their guidance and love. I offer reverence to Nature, which gifted us with the Great Lakes, oceans, trees, birds, forest and sea creatures, the sun, stars, and moon that all speak in sacred prose.

Foreword

by John Fox, PPM

Kronos, *Kairos* & Cupped Palms

When I met Terri Goslin-Jones, the very first conversations we explored were about time—and two specific ways of experiencing time: *Kronos,* which is linear, sequential, and determined by the clock, and *Kairos*, which is expansive, not ruled by the clock or calendar. Kairos allows us to flourish and thrive as we enter life moment by moment.

Terri and I were talking about the Poetic Medicine three-year and three-phase (Kronos!) training program and its requirements. Terri was speaking of her love for touching, I can truly say embracing, a way of living that is *felt* as linear time dissolves.

She wasn't resisting the time-necessary reality of doing the training. She wanted that. Rather, I was being made aware of how she, as if holding out her hands with palms forming a receptive cup, carries these experiences of different kinds of time in a lovely, simple intimacy.

As I write this Foreword some five years after that conversation, I am aware, as a teacher, what a privilege it was to be shown how important this is to Terri. What she shared has definitely informed my responses to her.

The truth is that Terri lives her truth. She, with great alacrity, very successfully completed the intensive three-year training to become a Practitioner of Poetic Medicine. She walked through this Kronos Time with commitment and humility, with courage and nobility.

I have deep admiration for her and for that.

That said, the image of her cupped palms has remained steadfast throughout. She keeps Kairos Time in the palm of her hand, connected to her heart. *Life's Concerto: Wholeness through Poetry and Expressive Arts* is the superb result.

Terri's poem *Shadow Speaks* is significant and represents something threaded throughout this book of poems. Terri declares here and elsewhere trust in the unknown and the capacity to find wisdom in the shadow. This was a way to arrive at that last line, *"Birth Your Holy Power."*

This Book is for your Exploration

If I am going to journey with someone to explore, even to touch my own healing needs, I want that guide to evoke in me trust of the unknown and my shadow. If you use this book for your own exploration, I believe that trust and the capacity to find wisdom will show themselves to you. This may not happen immediately; in fact, part of my trust comes from the slow unfolding.

When I read *Shadow Speaks* out loud to myself many times, these words rose to the surface of my heart:

    absorb   osmosis   drink
        learn   become
              savor

What could this mean? I gathered in a few words from Terri's poem (absorb and drink) and added the word osmosis. Poetry isn't that much of a Kronos-Time thing! I felt that by absorbing, I could learn. I was taking this poem in, as if by osmosis, and suddenly felt that I could become. Then to drink—in a felt-sense—I could savor!

These words rose creatively for me out of Kairos Time. Reading these poems out loud, with care and attention—yes, with intention, too—opens a path to Kairos. I want to encourage you to interact with these poems in this way. Allow them to be a catalyst for your own creativity.

This is one very good reason to recommend this book. As much as I honor poets we know and love (you can fill in their names here), I feel that within the covers of their books, there is a kind of impermeability. What I mean is that you can visit for a while, even exult and sigh deeply, but when you close the covers of that book, you have to go home with your memory.

The Voice in the Wilderness

Life's Concerto is written in such a way that it is a deep invitation for you to stay. The very structure of its seven themed sections acts like chapters in a book of life. Yet, there is something invitational and process oriented at work here that welcomes the reader.

There is a guest room in these pages, perhaps in a particular section (I kept returning to Section VI, Gardener of the Soul), in which you can go to rest, and then when the sun comes up, you may go to make tea in the kitchen. The pages will be open, and you will read on—slowly, of course.

This larger intention is expressed clearly in the excellent *Introduction* that Terri offers us. That's unusual in the general world of poetry books, but *Life's Concerto* is beautifully unusual; there is nothing general about it.

To write this Foreword, I made it a point to listen to a Great Course offered by the wonderful musicologist Robert Greenberg, PhD, titled *Concerto* (2006). In the first lecture, *The Voice in the Wilderness*, Greenberg says very early on by way of describing what a concerto is:

> It's got the individual solo voice...ringing forth against the mass of the orchestra, a metaphor for the individual solo voice ringing forth in the empowered individual reveling in his or her individuality.
>
> *
>
> Because of the singularity of the soloist's voice, the range and immediacy inherent in the concerto exceed that of every other type of music except opera.

I love the words "ringing forth" and the word "singularity." This is what Terri Goslin-Jones does here. Her singular and soloist voice rings forth—and she does this within the "mass of the orchestra" or in this important way, within the whole of Terri's life and the people in it, with light and dark, the natural world, and all the nuances of life and death that overflow herein.

Terri, setting the focus on concerto, says exactly that in the *Introduction*:

> Our life's musical composition includes our physical, intellectual, and spiritual realms, our families and all the people that enter our lives. Our story unfolds over the course of a lifetime within the musical composition of Nature—The Earth, and within a universal field.

One thing I treasure almost above everything is the sweet and profound affirmation that synchronicity offers us a confirmation of the universal field. I said that Robert Greenberg's first concerto lecture is titled *The Voice in the Wilderness*. In Section IV of this book, The Cracked Hallelujah, a poem titled *Dream Mirror* includes these very resonant and time-stopping lines:

> I long for my wilderness voice

*

> Let us speak to each other and make clear
> that we can grant each other grace to seize our wilderness
> voice.

As I have dedicated my whole life to further the possibilities of poetry-as-healer, those last three lines speak for the purpose of what this life means to me.

The deep synchronicity is that by calling her book of poems *Life's Concerto*, Terri's "longing for my wilderness voice" is wildly in tune with the deepest truth that Robert Greenberg sees, too.

Facing Heartbreak and the Felt Sense

I do not want to leave the impression that *Life's Concerto* is all about Kairos Time. It is also blessed with respect and love for what happens in Kronos time. That is, we all—Terri, each of you reading these poems, and I—will, one day die.

Death is by no means left out here. Authenticity must include facing heartbreak as expressed by loved ones dying, or it could be anyone. The acceptance of death gives these pages a true gravity that may bring you solace and permission to feel.

From time to time, Terri gives context to a poem. She writes and introduces her father's death graciously in the poem *"Where Did He Go?"*

> My father, Gerald Edward Goslin Sr. died of a heart attack
> when he was 48 years old. I was 24 and crossed a
> threshold into an internal realm and wrote this poem. His
> death imparted and gifted me with an understanding of
> impermanence and a desire to delve into consciousness
> and the mystery of life and death.

In reading a poem of another bracing loss, *Contemplation: My Mom's Death*, I find there is an intimacy and physicality that is creatively attractive in two ways—in the sense of its vivid, appealing imagery and a literal magnetic field that vibrates within the poem.

> I step outside my hermitage door,
> sit in the brown wicker chair
> on the riverbank
> wrapped in my velvet blanket.

> Tears of charism drop from my eyes.
> Sun-sliver peeks over a cloudy horizon.
> Sleepy, pinestraw trees awake on the riverbank.

The sensate physicality of these lines is evident in almost all of Terri's poems. Saying "Tears of charism drop from my eye" is a brilliant way of feeling, with abundance, that in her grieving, her tears carry the power of spiritual gifts. Her practice as an expressive arts educator includes the important words "felt sense." Those interested in this field of the healing expressive arts are ever in contact with the significance and centrality of that "felt sense" a person experiences. The peculiar thing is that even to write about the "felt sense" is a few steps away (at least) from that *experienced* felt sense!

Grief, in real-time, vibrates within the body and shakes the body as a felt sense; it is not a mental construct, decision, or choice. I encourage you to allow the imagery of these poems to touch you. I trust that they will also guide and teach. These insights are not arrived at rationally. You have to do the creative work unique to yourself that invites wakefulness to appear.

Life's Concerto is about Seeing

Life's Concerto is full of paradox and invitation. This may seem counter-intuitive: Who would knowingly enter into such an arrangement? You can find safety in these pages, even when a *Tornado Roars*,

> A voice whispers:
> Storms don't hurt the Sky.

You can also decide to let this volume of poems be a companion in the great adventure that life is, coming as it does with no guarantees—but an abundance of possibility and uncertainty:

> We must explore profound questions,
> not sure of anything or anyone.

My perspective as a poet puts my preoccupation with words. Yet, were I to allow myself that preoccupation, I would sorely miss another great dimension of this book. *Life's Concerto* is not only about reading. It is, in a very magnificent way, about *seeing*.

Terri's art, her photographs, her languages of color and form, visual symbols, and dream imagery demonstrate trust that is necessary and apparent in allowing the unconscious along with the superconscious to emerge. It is awesome and sheer pleasure that the art in this book is an expression of the "soloist" voice of Terri Goslin-Jones.

In closing my Foreword, I am going to circle back to this awareness as someone who taught and learned with Terri Goslin-Jones in this field of poetry therapy/poetic medicine. I am very appreciative that this book is more than a book of poems, more in that it is undergirded by therapeutic skill, consciousness, wisdom, and love.

Yes, I think Terri has gotten something quite strong from her Poetic Medicine training, and I know that she brought with her plenty of rich and excellent training and teaching, poem and artmaking, living and dying, being.

Kindness,

John Fox
Founder, The Institute for Poetic Medicine

Introduction

Life's Concerto: Wholeness through Poetry and Expressive Arts embodies my longstanding spiritual practice to utilize expressive arts to navigate undertows and transitions that surface in life. Poetry is an art form that opens doors to vulnerability and fosters empathy. In this book, I seek to understand universal issues that play out in life.

The key message of *Life's Concerto: Wholeness through Poetry and Expressive Arts* is that poetry provides an integrative and healing process that can transport us through the thresholds of life, providing an atlas for wise living and transformation. As I reveal the depth and intimacy of my life journey in the form of poems, I hope that you will feel inspired to engage deeply with poetry, too. If you already have an established poetry practice, perhaps this book will stir you to consider new ways of approaching and expanding your poetic expression.

Organization of the Book

The Introduction includes a theoretical foundation for poetry as medicine (Fox, 1995, 1997) and discusses how an expressive arts practice (Goslin-Jones et al. 2023; Knill & Atkins, 2021) can develop and enrich poetry. *Life's Concerto* presents my life experiences embodied through art. Poems and images are selected from my expressive arts practice to unveil the "music" or insights that arise during creative explorations.

A brief prose introduction launches Sections I–VII. Within each section readers are transported via poetry through a themed movement within my life story. In some ways, each life story is part of the universal story, and you may find parts of yourself expressed here.

Some poems, such as *Time Traveler, Dream Mirror,* and *A Mother's Vow,* recreate dream experiences that have deeply influenced my life. Other poems, such as *Tidal Waves, Mother Sea Turtle, Gathering Her Wits, Owl Medicine, Life on the Web,* and *Mississippi River Sunrise* describe encounters with Nature.

Poetry as a Creative Catalyst
and Devotion to Meaning-Making

I wrote this book because I believe that we are solo travelers with unique stories, and at the same time, we travel together as part of a universal field.

My poems arose from a desire to unravel paradoxes and mysteries that surfaced in my life. Engaging with poems offers a way to integrate life's fragments, share our stories, and discover broader perspectives. When we pay attention to our six senses, we can untangle life's experiences and expand our worldview.

Writing a poem is a way to cross over into an internal dwelling space and find puzzle pieces. This process deciphers messages that surface from encounters in life, including dreams, lessons from Nature, and exploring transpersonal realms. Poetry weaves fragments of life events and emotions into a visual tapestry. Stitching images and words together is a way to *re-envision* and integrate our lives into wholeness.

Creative Expression Births Meaning from Chaos

Poetry is a liaison between human and divine voices. *Life's Concerto* is composed of the music of my soul: expressions of a poetic voice that bears witness to the challenges and joys of experiencing an embodied, creative life. *The Oxford Dictionary* (May, 2018) defined a concerto as "A musical composition for a solo instrument or instruments accompanied by an orchestra, especially one conceived on a relatively large scale." Each of our stories can be written and sung as a poetic solo, and at the same time, we are accompanied by the large-scale orchestra of our life. Our life's musical composition includes our physical, intellectual, and spiritual realms, our families, and all the people who enter our lives. Our story unfolds over the course of a lifetime within the musical composition of Nature—the Earth, and within a universal field.

Moving through decades of life brings many changes and even chaos. We need effective, creative processes to make meaning from this turmoil and confusion. "In poetry, we can hold and honor the inexplicable mysteries of existence. Poetry is a threshold place of moving between the worlds of ordinary life, the imaginal realm, and the liminal space in between" (Knill & Atkins, 2021, p.132).

Poetry and Expressive Arts

The foundation of my creative practice embraces person-centered expressive arts and Natalie Rogers's work with the *Creative Connection*. (Rogers, 1997, 2011). The connection between and the ways that art forms influence each other is endless. The *Creative Connection* includes meditation, movement, music, artmaking, and writing for the purpose of inquiry and self-expression.

I have been part of a Creative Spirit Circle with five other members since 2011. Together, we wrote *Weaving Ourselves Whole: A Guide to Forming a Transformational Expressive Arts Circle* (Goslin-Jones et al., 2023). Poetry is part of our circle process; we read and write poems, and at times, we develop collaborative poems.

There is a structure and process that supports our creative expression. Within our Creative Spirit Circle and my solo expressive arts practice, a candle is lit, and there is 1) meditation, 2) authentic movement/gestures, 3) spontaneous artmaking, 4) expressive writing, and 5) dialogue.

Reading and writing poetry are essential to my creative expression. I collect and savor poems that have touched me with an electrical current. As I contemplate their sounds, a rhythm opens inside of me. I enter what I call Kairos Time. I travel beyond chronological time and enter the mystery of Divine Time. This may be experienced as a deepening of presence. I experience Kairos Time as a current that carries me across space and beyond time zones.

Oftentimes, I translate my art into a poem, giving the artwork a voice. As I examine the metaphor suggested by the visual work, I feel stretched and transported by the intuitive logic of the metaphor. The visual art and prose become a vital container for my emotional landscape. When I enter the magnetic field of poetry, I converse with my outer and inner worlds, and the harmony of my soul expands within my human body. Writing is more than self-expression; it becomes an encounter with creative energy and another way of knowing something greater than oneself.

Creative expression in all the arts is about *not knowing* and then delving into unknown territory. The creative process combines elements of nature that are internal and external. McNiff (2015), in *Imagination in Action: Secrets for Unleashing Creative Expression,* described creativity as a "force of nature that permeates all things" (p. 10). There is an alchemical healing process that occurs in artmaking. Obstacles and turmoil can be transformed into new life by reshaping life's complexities into artistic forms (McNiff, 2023).

In an expressive arts practice, movement, music, and artmaking expand sensory awareness and unlock creative energy. Oftentimes, when a person participates in physical movement, experiences music, or creates art, new emotions and ideas come to light (Rogers, 1997, 2011). Writing supports the assimilation of the puzzle pieces that arise when we are open to not knowing. When expressive arts are synthesized with writing prose and poetry, verbal expression facilitates a deeper understanding and absorption of the inner experience (Goslin-Jones, 2020; Goslin-Jones et al., 2023).

For example, when I focus on sensory details during writing, I decode my life experiences into imagery and words. At the same time, I gain new perspectives and expand my personal and world view. It is as if I first look through a close-up lens, then shift to a wide-angle lens to assimilate the whole landscape. Writing empowers me to reflect upon, give voice to, and assimilate wisdom emerging from my mind, body, and spirit. The poem becomes a sanctuary that holds the expression of life's spiritual experiences in ways that complement and build upon my expressive arts practice. This creative discipline weaves together inner fragments and fosters equanimity even during seasons of distress.

Therapeutic Benefits of Expressive Arts & Poetry

Engaging with the arts can provide emotional clarity as we go through life's challenges. The exploration of visual arts, dance, drama, and writing offers a process to develop emotional clarity. The imaginative range is enhanced through expressive arts, and an enriched crystallization of emotional material develops. A deeper mind–body connection is formed from the artistic encounter (Knill, Barba & Fuchs 2004, 2015).

In their book *Poetry in Expressive Arts: Supporting Resilience through Poetic Writing, Margo Knill and Sally Atkins* (2021), educators and poets, delved into multiple dimensions of poetry, including writing, reading, performing, speaking, and listening for the purposes of supporting resilience and healing and unlocking the imaginative realm. They discussed how poetry can "build resilience and create hope and confidence as a platform for healing, reconciliation, problem-solving and personal and professional development" (p. 27).

Poetry is a form of arts-based research that includes new ways of exploring, knowing, and being. Poetic learning explores what may be foreign, strange, and even mysterious. A poet begins to explore this with just one word, and this process unfolds into multiple words that express new meanings. There are layered steps in the poetic process, and the cumulative impact may open the poet to experiences of beauty, surprise, mystery, and awe.

Poetic Medicine

How does poetry lead to cultivating wholeness and living a life that is more whole and complete? Life is filled with contradictions. Poetry supports the logical mind with intuition, metaphor, images, and rhythms, thus allowing us to observe uncomfortable paradoxes. "Poetry is a natural medicine; it is like a homeopathic tincture derived from the stuff of life itself—your experience" (Fox, 1995, p. 3). Poetry becomes a doorway into discovering "the connection between our life and what exists beyond us, we recognize how we are related to each other, to all of creation, to the unknown. And knowing this will help heal us" (Fox, 1995 p. 55).

The Institute of Poetic Medicine (IPM), founded by John Fox in 2005, is dedicated to awakening soulfulness in the human voice. IPM offers a wide variety of tools to heal the body, mind, and spirit. These resources include poetry workshops, training programs, educational materials, poetry books, and a community of poets (Institute of Poetic Medicine, 2023; https://www.poeticmedicine.org).

Reading and writing poetry connects us to our interior world and to a community of kindred spirits. Poem-making embodies the pain and passion of life by connecting our heads and hearts. Vast experiences are distilled, and disparate fragments are captured into something novel and surprising. Poetry speaks to us in code by using metaphor, sound, color, feelings, and images. Furthermore, the metaphors and musical notes we experience in poetry expand the way we perceive ourselves and the world around us (Fox, 1995). Reading and writing poems are medicine and a therapeutic practice for healing that can be shared with a therapist, trusted friend, or within a poetry circle (Fox, 1995, 1997).

Kim Rosen, author of *Saved by a Poem,* discussed how poems change and heal a person. She believes that poetry changes the brain. For example, our breath and heartbeat respond to vibrations from speaking and listening to poetry. Rosen vowed,

> As you embody the poems you love, you may meet yourself, your imagination, and your true voice in ways you never dreamed of. As you speak the words aloud, you can change the world around you with poetry's medicine—dissolving lines of separation, fostering intimacy and awakening the heart. (2009, p. xix)

Poetry is a living event that needs to be embodied, felt, and spoken out loud. When we connect our inner landscape to our outer world, words take shape on the page and become secret messages. The same words have the potential to contact each reader and yet vibrate with different sounds and hold distinct messages for each person receiving the poem.

The Natural World as Confidante and Mentor

The natural world is a guide to my inner landscape. *Life's Concerto: Wholeness through Poetry and the Expressive Arts* reflects my spiritual relationships with the ocean, moon, trees, plants, animals, and seasonal changes. Archetypes and images drawn from Nature and from my inner world inform my poetry and reveal how "Nature is my survival guide." I have been comforted and guided by trees, by massive sea turtles returning to the sea, by the presence of owls and other creatures. Paying close attention to the natural world has helped me adapt and grow while traveling through childhood, mid-life, and now, as I enter elderhood.

Nature teaches us about life's natural flow. The natural world holds rhythm, pattern, and music. As we witness a sunrise, sunset, flood, hurricane, or tornado, we encounter dynamic change and fresh perspectives. There are times when change is so abrupt that it shakes the Earth. Nevertheless, Nature can teach us how to survive and thrive through the rugged waves that penetrate our lives.

Purpose of this Book

Life's Concerto harvests lessons from daily living and from my professional immersion in humanistic, transpersonal, and depth psychology. This book uses artistic inquiry to cultivate a contemplative practice that explores universal themes. *Life's Concerto* is designed for poets, expressive arts practitioners, counselors, educators, psychologists, therapists, and those interested in developing a creative practice for the purpose of growth and self-actualization.

Summary

Ultimately, writing is a mindfulness practice. It can be an expansive dive into a hidden world. It can even serve the purpose of discovering how to live a meaningful life amidst layers of mystery. This takes courage and curiosity.

My mission as a poet is to explore life's sacred encounters. "Poetic sensibility discerns the deepest need and brings forth images to speak the unspeakable, and to render the invisible world accessible" (Hollis, 2000, p. 54). Through our archetypal imagination, we birth divine energy, healing the tension of opposites and expressing our experience through art. When the vastness of the human experience is communicated in symbol and metaphor, new ways of knowing emerge through the poet's voice. Poets bear witness, praise, and express their experience of meaning (Hollis, 2000).

This book shares poems about childhood, mid-life, marriage, being a parent, family member, teacher, researcher, life-long learner, and universal sojourner. As I travel through the decades of my life, my poetic voice encompasses chronological events, and simultaneously, I transcend ordinary time and enlarge my awareness of spiritual time.

In *Life's Concerto,* I explore how poetry can be a therapeutic process that supports physical, emotional, and spiritual growth. When a poem is shared, we become interconnected through the resilience and vibrancy of sharing our human nature. It is my hope that exploring poetry and expressive arts will expand your creative expression. As you read this book and write your own poems, may you experience the alchemy and music of your life.

References

Fox, J. (1995). *Finding what you didn't lose. Expressing your truth and creativity through poem-making.* Jeremy P. Tarcher-Putman.

Fox, J. (1997). *Poetic medicine: The healing art of poem-making.* Jeremy P. Tarcher-Putnam.

Goslin-Jones, T. (2020). Expressive arts. In M. Runco & S. Pritzker (Eds.), *Encyclopedia of creativity* (3rd ed., pp. 478–484). Academic Press.

Goslin-Jones, T., Caraffa, P., Carson, H., McCallum, K., Reinert, G., & Willinger, N., (2023). *Weaving ourselves whole: A guide to forming a transformational expressive arts circle.* University Professors Press.

Greenberg, R. (2006). *The concerto,* audio CD. The Teaching Company.

Hollis, J. (2000). *The archetypal imagination.* Texas A & M University Press.

Knill, M., & Atkins, S. (2021). *Poetry in expressive arts: Supporting resilience through poetic writing.* Jessica Kingsley Publishers.

Knill, P., Barba, H., & Fuchs, M. (2004). *Minstrels of soul.* EGS Press.

McNiff, S. (2015*). Imagination in action: Secrets for unleashing creative expression.* Shambala.

McNiff, Shaun. (2023). An integral community of art and healing: Transcending silos in the ecological era. *Journal of Applied Arts & Health.* 14. 13–25. 10.1386/jaah_00124_1.

Oxford Dictionary *(*May 21, 2018). https://www.encyclopedia.com/literature-and-arts/performing-arts/music-theory-forms-and-instruments/concerto.

Rogers, N. (1997). *The creative connection: Expressive arts as healing.* Science & Behavior Books.

Rogers, N. (2011). *The creative connection for groups: Person-centered expressive arts for healing and social change.* Science and Behavior Books.

Rosen, K. (2009). *Saved by a poem: The transformative power of words.* Hay House.

Section I

What Sides of Myself Need to be Heard?

"What is most personal is most universal."
—Carl Rogers

Escuchar is a Spanish verb that means to listen with the ears of the heart. Many facets of life are difficult to understand and need a special kind of listening. Poetry and artwork are ways that I listen with my heart to reveal messages from life's mysteries. Within my interior realm, I witness a multitude of voices and creative resources, including archetypal energy from my child, artist, mother, and mystic. Writing poetry and making art help me to understand that it takes a lifetime to recognize the depth and potential of our fuller identity.

This section welcomes the poet and reader. I invite you to slow down, take a breath, and open to an *"Inner Neighborhood."* Prepare a contemplative place within your home for your creative process. Bring your favorite beverage, light a candle, your notebook, and an art journal. Then find an introspective place inside yourself. Dwell in this quiet space to inquire, *"What Sides of Myself Need to Heard?"*

Sleep to Wake

Secret words,
buried in the fabric
of my soul.

Veiled words,
vibrate in a foreign tongue.

Jailed words,
hide in the cave of my heart,
embalmed and swathed,
and sleeping alone.

Is an unspoken
word
a hostage
or a sage?

What Sides of Myself Need to be Heard?

Emotions are housed in my body,
boarders sometimes avoided and feared.
Rebellion, anxiety, anger, and heartache,
live next door to happiness, freedom, and ease.

Each and every one of these tenants,
are sound asleep and take refuge,
sheltered in separate chambers
of my beating heart.

My Mystic, my Mother,
my Artist, my Child,
crave space and a place
to wake up and be witnessed.

How can I converse
through the course of a lifetime
with these paradoxical parts of myself?

And unearth wisdom
that yearns to be heard.

Close In

Lean in to find my voice
the truthful place to start
is near my treasured heart.

I'm not ready to share.

Scrambled words are my guests
the visitors that I hear
are bees buzzing in my ears.

Tonight, let my body sleep
tender space to listen deep
baby steps into the night.

Inner Neighborhood

Icy cold in Michigan,
Sunnyview School closed early.
She walked home from kindergarten,
black boots squeaking in the snow.

In her internal neighborhood,
she could go anywhere desired
with her imaginary friends.

She forgot to wear her mittens,
but she was on an adventure.
Wandering along new sideroads,
to search for her brother on safety patrol.

Her big brother was nowhere in sight.
All the children had disappeared,
in the icy cold daylight.

Her stomach twirled up and down,
her fingers lost their feelings,
her cheeks felt slippery wet.

Where was her brother,
who was going to walk her home?

The little girl
did not know where to go.

A nice man stopped his car.
Her clothes were soaked,
her hands so cold,
he would take her home, he said.

She pondered for a moment,
heard her mother say,
"Do not talk to strangers and
never climb in a car for a ride."

Life's Concerto

She declined his offer
and he drove away.

Then she returned
to her inner neighborhood,
and sought a beloved friend.

She invited her wise Guide
to come out and play.
Walking side by side
they found their way home.

Throughout the rest of her life
she returned to her wise Guide
to find her way home—
again and again and again.

Creative Quest

I.
Sometimes, I am
a quick-change artist

Sometimes, I am
a wise artist:
sage, seeker, seer

Sometimes, my outside and inside match.
Sometimes, they do not.

Sometimes,
I try to achieve what others need,
unflappable on the outside. While inside
a Critic exiles and buries
my wild child,
who yearns to create.

My fractured spirit craves expression.
Messy minds, gritty fingerprints,
marks deeply embedded
in each crack, crevice,
and silky surface of life.

confusion
rocking
rolling
messy
scratching
stretching

my wild child rouses
angry, exhausted, wounded,
crammed with shame and pain.

II.

My Wise One unveils
tempura paints with gigantic brushes

and proclaims…

Why wait for perfect moments?

Breathe in all shades of the rainbow,
choose all the screaming colors,
paint your lifescape
with vibrant brushstrokes.

This *is* the magical moment:
Do what you want
be who you are…
Reveal vast feelings
look, listen, taste, smell, touch, twirl.

Unbolt
your inner threshold,
squeeze through the tight door,
eavesdrop inside the underworld.

Dear One, you are safe
to create.

Longing is the Music of my Soul

*An ensemble of musicians and a choir
inhabit my inner chambers—*

To compose the music of your soul
unlock the door to spirit's longing.

Open the doors and windows,
unearth silence within your heartroom,
let spiritual desires surge.

To compose the music of your soul
gaze forward and
forget what was learned.

Pay attention to life's essence
not to what was earned.

To compose the music of your soul
forget what is behind you,
forget what has been unsaid.

Breathe in the concerto of your life
heed the juicy season rising,
say yes to not knowing.

Take flight and leave Kronos behind
cross the threshold.

Let spirit's gale blow through—
soar to Kairos clouds,
perch beyond the stream of time.

Letter from my Magical, Mystical Guide

Dear One,

Feast on the crack of dawn
arise, inhale, and breathe
the salty air that roared in
from the universe last night

Earth speaks to you in
secret, sacred prose

Within the deep-sea upsurge
mysterious creatures emerge
one by one, and yet they
dwell in community

Roam on life's seashore
visit these mysteries and treasures
crabs, turtles, starfish, and stingrays
bathed and sent by the mermaids

In this lifetime, sail as:
curly-haired child, rebel teen,
lover, wife, mother, gardener,
teacher, artist, mystic, and poet

Dwell in your
magical beach house
sprinkle stardust
on your mud floors
now is the time

to cross through
an enchanted gate

There is still more
through that door –
in the supper of life
the sunset arrives

Travel through this passageway
open gateways
disguised with rising vines

Fly through the needle's eye
soar through the threshold into the sea
listen to ancient ways
swim in the underworld
seize treasures

When you were young,
you forgot

As you grow, you remember—
secrets
of the ocean breakers
heartache and devotion

This is why… charism of tears
fall from your eyes
like ocean drops from the sky
into the wide-open briny
sea of life:

To see
To be

Section II

Tidal Waves

"Nature is made to conspire with spirit to emancipate us."
—Ralph Waldo Emerson

There is a landscape outside of us and a landscape inside of us. For most of my life I have made annual sojourns to the Great Lakes or the ocean. Now, I spend several months a year living with the ocean. On January 1 of each year, I plunge into the Atlantic Ocean to wake up my body and spirit. I swim with the waves as they rise and fall.

The word *nature* is derived from the Latin word *Natus,* to become. In *Tidal Waves,* I connect with Nature to gather strength in the midst of life's stormy waves. Nature offers sustenance and guidance. Newborn energy enters my body. The poems in this section reveal some of my encounters with the ocean, birds, and sea creatures. When I interact with the natural world, something happens inside: A doorway opens, and the landscape of my interior world expands.

Daybreak at Seabrook Island

Walk across wooden bridge,
ocean path bathed in rising dawn.
Cast sandals aside, spread beach towel
upon sparkling, dewy sand.

I am...
solo traveler at half past five in early May,
body bathed in breeze.
Raspberry stripes splash the shoreline,
the ocean is my passageway.

Weave with the waves.
As ocean breakers leap,
lunar tide baptizes me.
Brown pelicans nosedive,
catching delectable breakfast.

Wander with the sunrise,
roam on the ocean's drifting path,
embossed with sand steps.

Unbound time rises.

Little Tree of Life

Ocean whitecaps washed up
Little Tree from the sea.

Imagine,
if this pocket-size tree could tell me
what is buried deep in the sea.

What if I could swim
into the underworld,
where Little Tree dwelled?

Imagine,
if Little Tree could tell me
what was buried inside of me.

Can I dream,
with Little Tree and the sea,
travel through a portal
to truly see
into mystery—

Mother Sea Turtle

The ocean is in our blood, we
return to the sea instinctively,
just like the ancient sea turtle.

I.
Magnetic Ocean
calls her name
heavy and ancient
she pulls Earth's energy
into her mandala body.

Swept onto the beach
by the sea's moonlight
she traverses the ocean and
tiptoes to land.

Mother Sea Turtle -300 pounds
crawls laboriously
drags her ancient shell
collapses
between miraculous breaths.

Digging a birth nest
two feet deep
on sandy earth beach,
she drops 100 eggs
one by one
safely buried.

II.
How is it possible,
to breathe on land
and breathe in the sea?

She holds her breath
while swimming
deep into the mystery…
Mother Sea Turtle
surfaces from depths

of her dream life
to birth
future generations.

She crawls by the moon
and crosses land to sea,
belly-heart caresses
Mother Earth's pulse.

Using every ounce of energy
in her prehistoric body,
she returns to the ocean
from which she arose.

Floating on her belly shell
the sea trail carries her
back to the depths
of her prehistoric
being—

Poetic Promise
An ocean roars through my body

Stand Still
Calm the waters within.
Attune to your inner ocean.
Stroll to the shoreline
linger on the gritty sand.
Spill your cup of worry.
Take notes from the whispering wind.
Your Sacred One
breathes wisdom.

Ocean Tides Chant

Brown pelicans glide
and sashay in the breeze

Ocean breakers broadcast a tune:
Like the ancient sea turtle
I was raised on stormy waves.
Deepsea whisper summons me
to receive peace in between the turbulence.

I yearn to swim in the ocean's wisdom
with ancient, hidden creatures

Myriad of dialects humming in the deep-sea
submerged mysteries drift ashore

I imagine through osmosis
sea, land, and sky

unite in the tide of my body
In this mesmerizing way

The universe and I intertwine
to dwell in this miraculous moment

Tidal Waves

While falling in and out of sleep—
waves of emotion
crash through my body.

I live in an ocean

Tidal breakers sweep from
my feet to my gut and
connect me to primordial waters.

Dreaming in murky water,
I struggle to understand life's dis-ease.
Anxiety floods my river veins.

Waves cascade all night long

A shadow whispers,
*All rivers wash back into the ocean
and unite with primordial water.*

At daybreak, hearing the
tides crash against the coastline,

I wander down the boardwalk
through sweetgrass dunes,
sandy beach comforts my bare feet.

Rhythm from the ocean's breath
soothes my body. I wade into water
and swim deeper and deeper.

Floating on my back into the sea, I
drift further and further, as I listen
to the underworld's symphony.

Let tidal waves and the ocean current
carry me where they may.

II. Tidal Waves

Sacred Depth

My soul cries for comfort.
Chronic sorrow engulfs
the cave of my heart.

Silence
unlocks Spirit's door.

Soul tides crash
to the surface.
Undercurrents plunge and soar.

Silence
summons me
to return to my Source.

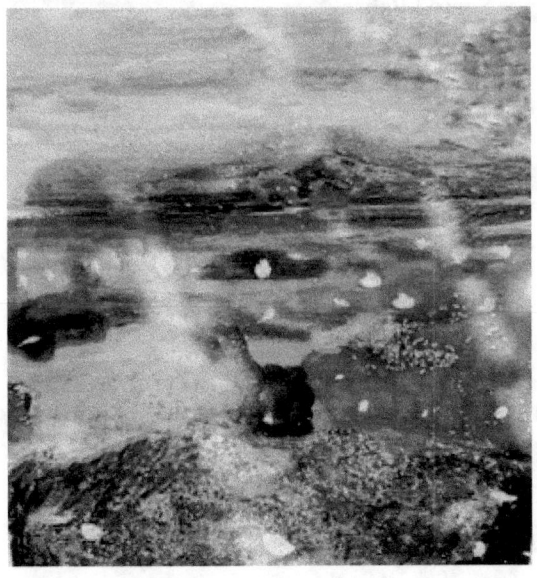

Whispering Wind
An ekphrastic painting and poem for my brother Tod

Wind whispers—
it is time to leave

Bare feet climb sweetgrass dunes
footprints engrave silver sand

Threshold candles glow
guiding your journey
into golden shoreline

Wind whispers—
it is time to leave

Sacred Pause

Breathless

Heart adjourns

Footprints
wash away

Boundless

You travel
through a deep-sea portal
into radiant sky

Life's Concerto

Transcendent Tides

I.
My lifeboat spins like a haywire compass,
my heart is crushed.
A knock bangs
on my boat's door.
If I don't *answer*, I might capsize.

I take a chance... Unbolt the door,
plunge through a river tunnel
and struggle against red tides.

Swimming through
swirling waterways,
I listen to the flowing waters.
I must consent.
Let transcendent tides
carry me where they may.

II.
Finally,
my lifeboat and I reunite
to reground
spiritual energy.

My inner life and outer life
realign and intertwine.
My body expands to embrace my spirit.

III.
A river of joy opens inside me,
I seize a moment to sip warm cinnamon tea,
then sit and pray with
sweetgrass,
and listen to Sandpipers chant.

I see my Spirit Sister's seeds sprout,
I feel our Family Soul ripen.

I hear wisdom whispered from the wind's current.
The river of joy opens inside of me.

IV.
What has changed?

My heart is stitched back together,
embroidered with the river's red threads.

Mystical hope opened my heart.
Mystical love surrounds me.

Even though my heart was crushed
and my bones worn thin, my body expands
to embrace my spirit.

Beneath life's lost dreams,
we travel together.
circling our lifeboats
to discover our collective star map.

Sleeping rhythms shift, our bodies rouse,
we witness patterns in the dark sky.
Now, we see in ancient ways and
read our compass by the light of the moon.
Our star map compass guides us
into uncharted waters and back to land.
We awaken within the Lamp of Mystical Love.

V.
Look outward… thousands of candles light our river path.
Our vision expands.
Look upward… thousands of constellations light our sky path.
Star maps guide our voyage.

We are not alone.

Section III

Time to Turn: Ancient Monastery

"My imagination is a monastery and I am its monk."
—John Keats

Life presents many unexpected experiences. We are challenged on how to meet them and live them. These shifts and undercurrents take a toll on daily living and create confusion. We become perplexed, we don't know how to make changes and may feel trapped. Frequently, it isn't obvious when it is *Time to Turn* or time to embrace transitions.

When doors slam shut and I feel stuck, I crack open a door into my inner world to reflect and seek guidance. I call this place my *Inner Monastery*, where there are multiple rooms for contemplation and exploration. I imagine I am traveling through an interior labyrinth to dialogue with life's mysteries. This is the place where I can hear the melody and rhythm of my life.

Contemplation is a pathway to inner guidance, a way to unearth clarity and co-create our life's direction. Creative energy can emerge from adverse situations. This creative process requires time in the world to experience life and time to retreat into an inner sanctuary for discernment.

Time to Turn

Eavesdrop
inside life's tides.
Surf liminal lanes to
grapple with questions,
scattered across the spectrum.

Betwixt and between streets.

Orbit secret corridors
between bewildered paths.
I long for an empty boulevard,
I crave a stop sign,
I ache for sacred space.

Lamplights flicker,
fog blinds me.
Moon shadow summons.

Wordless
motionless,
uncertain,
tangled in a web.

Until, *that* voice sings to me.

Soul's music of the night,
glides through the
eye of the needle,
to speak to me.

Should I turn,
should I stay,
should I adjourn?

Can I see,
am I blind,
from the chaos
of frenetic days?

Desire solitude
desire stillness
desire silence.

Monastic life
beckons me
to be
free.

Tree of Life Hermitage

I snuggle into my monastic nest,
Mississippi River floats by.
Ten degrees of icy wind currents,
encircle *Tree of Life* hermitage.

On the wall hangs a painting
with a figure that walks on water.
Yellow roses enchant a cherry vase.
Floor heater defrosts my doorway.

Dressed in flannel pajamas
wool army socks, and fluffy slippers,
I wrap my velvet blanket around my body,
and shift into contemplation.

Time passes, a doorway opens
inviting a sacred pause.
I listen and descend further
to receive messages …

Soul defrosts a window
into my heart space

Finally, I remember:
moment by moment
breath by breath
transports spirit

Inhabit this footpath
shaped by each step,
breath by breath

Descend and then,
listen…

Ascend and then,
walk with presence…

Passageway to the soul—

III. Time to Turn: Ancient Monastery

Ancient Monastery

My sacred heart
contains an iron gate,
a lock and key.

An engraved brass bolt,
shields my heart chamber.

When life is treacherous,
the iron gate slams shut
to safeguard my heart.

I descend a staircase,
thousands of candles
ignite my exodus.
Chimes echo…
cardinals chant.
Ballads of hope arise.

I cross a threshold,
lost to outer life.

Interior corridors
reveal tranquil chambers
enveloped in love
within my ancient monastery.

Surrender

Everything is falling apart
moment by moment.
Show me, universe
how to find peace
when everything is falling apart.
Show me, universe
how to dream my dreams
when everything is falling apart.
Show me, universe
how to hold myself together
and dwell inside the question.
Surrender and desire merge
when everything is falling apart.

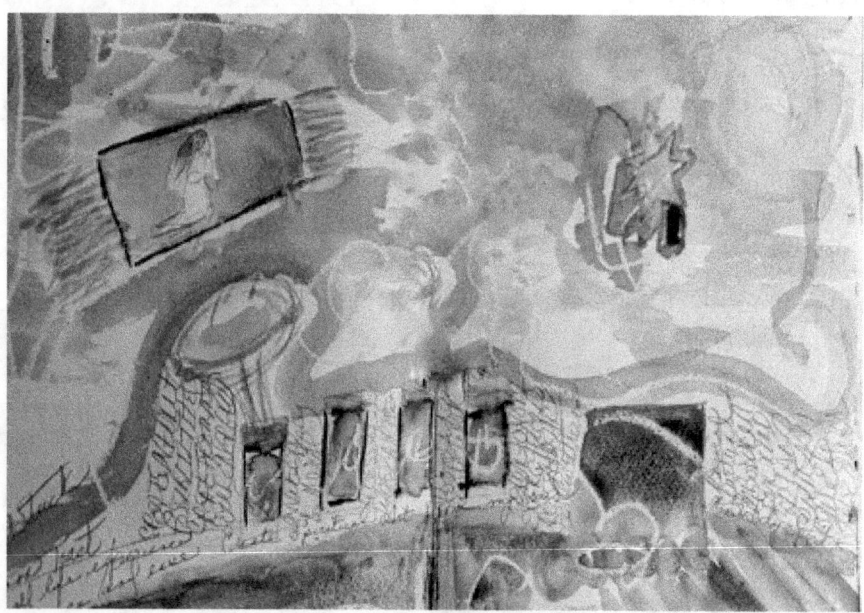

Ash Mystery

"In this brief transit a dream-crossed twilight between birth and dying." —T.S. Eliot

Trees liberate their leaves,
organic greeneries decompose
and crumble under my feet,
as I walk through life's equinox
what once was green is now ash.

Earth's ashes
smudged across
my third eye.

Heaven and Earth
cross each other
on my forehead.

Is there a god?

Embers smolder
on my temple.

From dust I came
to dust I return.

My body becomes
a threshold
for spirit to journey
from my third eye,
opening my heart.

I cross over —
Into mystical time.

Shadow Speaks

Unearth the midnight
of your soul's mystery.

Push through the darkness,
trudge through the underworld.

Trust your journey.

Drink shadow and light,
until you absorb
the sacred night.

Fulfill your destiny
and bring forth light.
Return with a blessing.

Birth your holy power.

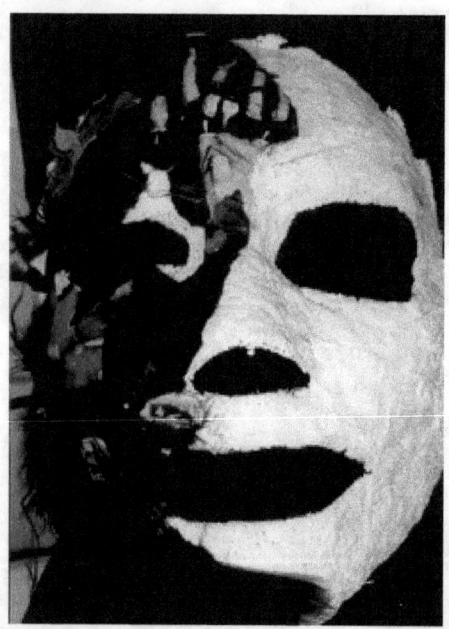

Crossing Over

I pray to Silver Moon
as I entrust my mother, 87
to the luminous snowy night
in Saginaw, Michigan.

Please, walk her home.

Two steps forward,
two steps backward.
Travel the winding, sodden road,
tread through fallen pine trees
to take the long way home.

Please walk with her
during this last snowfall,
don't drift into dubious ditches.

Her path is made by walking,
through this last passing season,
that some people call death.

Let heaven unfold
it's all around her.

Take the long way home.

Let the snow melt,
beneath the Silver Moon.

Sip and savor snow spirit's breath,
as she ponders these next steps.

*You just have to let go— and
take the long way home...*

Let heaven unfold.

III. Time to Turn: Ancient Monastery

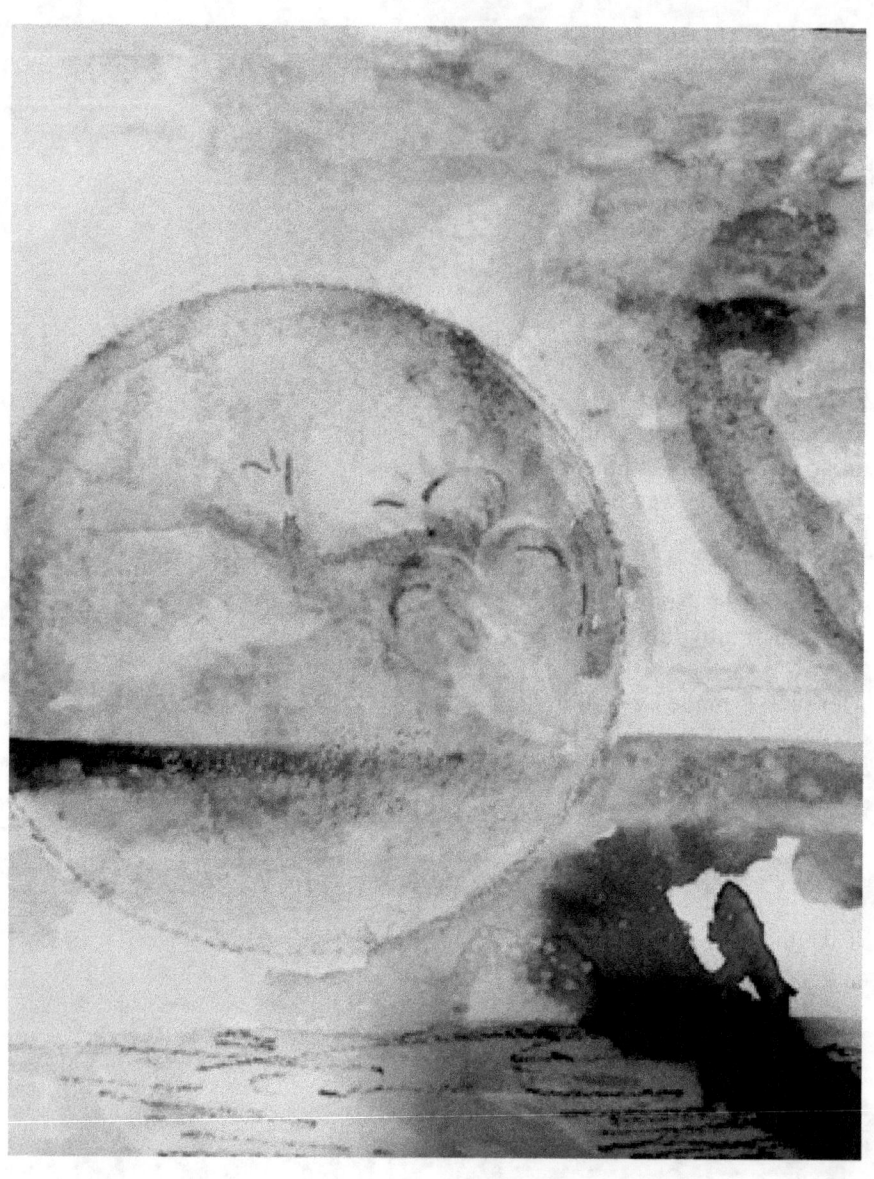

Contemplation: My Mom's Death

Scattered thoughts…

I am now an Earth orphan.
No mom, no dad on this Earth.
Trees and rivers and the ocean
are my home.

From my window
at the *Tree of Life* hermitage,
I see a flock of eagles nestle
in my White Oak river tree.

Other eagles soar high
and low, and I witness
Mississippi River miracles:

I ask:
"Mom, are you here?
Can you let me know?
Please send a message."

I shuffle, shuffle, shuffle
a deck of angel and saint cards.
Pick three, turn them over,
spread them onto the twin bed.
The angels speak:
Mother
Heaven
Faith.

My mom says,
"I am here, have faith."

Who needs words?
I step outside my hermitage door,
sit in the brown wicker chair
on the riverbank
wrapped in my velvet blanket.

Tears of charism drop from my eyes.
Sun-sliver peeks over a cloudy horizon.
Sleepy, pinestraw trees awake on the riverbank.

Chilly winds blow my curly, graying hair.
An eagle whistles and watches over me.

Train tracks click, railroad rumbles.
River barge blasts its horn.
Mississippi River carries the barge's echo,

reminding me to pause,
heed this sacred space.

I descend deeper into my chair,
into my being
and listen to the river's rhythm —

Vision of Peace, St. Louis, Missouri
View from *Tree of Life Hermitage* room

Section IV

The Cracked Hallelujah

"I have woven a parachute out of everything broken."
—William Stafford

We have no idea what will emerge across our lifetime. No one comes into life wanting to sign up for the intense challenges that life generates. The poems in *The Cracked Hallelujah* connect to complex realms, including addiction, death, dream life, and grief.

Life's overwhelming situations must be faced head on. *The Cracked Hallelujah* tells stories about entering the underworld and finding strength to return to daily living and thrive in surprising ways. Human nature holds tremendous potential. As we travel through life, we take on different roles to express our creative potential. It is natural that some parts of our potential are suppressed while other parts evolve. Even so, there is a *Wild One* inside that says, "Don't give up these unique and essential parts of who you are meant to become."

Time Traveler

Surfing on sleep waves
I drift through dreamland,

Wander inbound
to seek music of the night.

Door knock summons,
pounding vibration
shakes my body.

Creative spirit barges into my room—
to deliver a 3 a.m. decree:

Wake up
Rise up
Float into spirit time

I abandon my Earth anchor
and soar

Where am I?
Who am I?
Why am I here?

I skydive and drop
through a black hole,
into dazzling darkness.

What part of me is lost?
What part is found?

Dream Mirror

As we look into the dream mirror
we are more than ourselves. We
are simultaneously here
and yet we are over there.

Deep in sleep, I journey
through a tunnel, a path, a shimmering sea
as a cyclone of energy swirls through me:
Where am I going?

I enter an underground wilderness.
A stranger appears to answer my call.
He invites me to sit beside him on a bench.
Our vision expands as we marvel at the sights.

Diamonds glisten from the ocean's mirror,
exposing the midnight sky. Gusty waves reveal
dolphins leaping from the mysterious sea.
Moonbeams light up my curiosity.

The man beside me suddenly
embraces a cat-like creature. It turns
and bites me. Its sandpaper tongue licks
and scrapes the top of my hand.

Startled, I try to pull away
but the creature's tongue is glued to my skin.
My hand throbs as I try to escape. Frozen
throat shouts in a whisper:

Help me! Help me!
is all I can utter.
Though in pain, I try to take it all in,
to understand
what is happening.

Life's Concerto

Using all my muscular force
I tumble back through a time tunnel
with the shadow creatures of midnight.
Scream pierces the darkness: Help me! Help me!

My husband leaps, with the shock wave
turns me over; I crash-land on my side.
Slowly, I grasp where I am.

I want to swim back to this barrier island.
Cross over—into shadowland,
where the creatures shock and provoke me,
where I enter another state of being.

All day long, I try to understand.

It takes hours to return to ordinary time,
to gather myself. Exhausted from my travels
in this faraway, mysterious place,
I long for my wilderness voice.

Finally, a message sails through my mind:

We are here, and yet we are over there.
As we look into the dream mirror
we are more than ourselves.

Let us speak to each other and make clear
that we can grant each other
grace to seize our wilderness voice.

As we look into the dream mirror
we are more than ourselves. We
are simultaneously here
and yet we are over there.

IV. The Cracked Hallelujah

Where Did He Go?

My father is gone,
but he didn't say goodbye.

These feelings of mine
are locked up inside.

God, what is your plan?
Did you take him with you?

Will I see him again?

It makes me so sad,
everything I didn't say.

My heart is in a knot
I don't understand.

My father is gone.

Note: My father, Gerald Edward Goslin Sr., died of a heart attack when he was 48 years old. I was 24 and crossed a threshold into an internal realm and wrote this poem. His death imparted and gifted me with an understanding of impermanence and a desire to delve into consciousness and the mystery of life and death.

Reverse Birthing

I.
I sit
beside my brother
in his hospice bed.

We grew up together
side by side —brother and sister.
In my eyes, he had a broken life:
two divorces, penniless, a hermit.

In his eyes, he had a right life:
Mensa scholar,
truck driver, mechanic, dad,
dreamer and stargazer.

Minute by minute,
day by day,
for 14 months
releasing life.

My brother is vanishing,
100 pounds fade away
and still, he preserves
his awareness.

Trying to prove
consciousness
survives the body.

II.
Reclining on a cot
beside my brother,
I hold his hand.
He is letting go.

I speak
*"We are together
in a birthing process."*

Life's Concerto

He responds, "*In reverse.*"
we smile and know
exactly what each other means.

Summer in Saginaw, Michigan.
My brother in his hospice bed,
scorching room
with a sizzling heater
oxygen machine hissing.

I unbolt the window.

A midsummer muggy night
the window cracked open;
my heart breaks open.
Holding on and letting go.

Reverse birthing…

Family Roots
"It didn't start with you," —Mark Wolman

I.
I stand in a long line of family farmers,
red flannel shirts and blue jean overalls.
In our billowing Saginaw countryside,
acres of corn die a thousand deaths.
Combine harvesters cut corn rows down,
and chop kernels off the cob.
Crown roots left behind gather nutrients from dark dirt,
to fertilize soil for future generations.

Along with seeds sown in our cornfields,
thousands of family stories
are buried in our backyard.
Periodically, we burn these fields
to remove weeds and prevent disease.

Family history and family futures dwell
side by side in these flaming fields.

Abruptly, addiction storms into our family's living room,
grabs hold and shrouds our home.
Down pillows of grass rise in holy flames—
a boundless prairie of grief.

II.
Long before dawn,
storm clouds knock together in my body.
Fog surges from my feet through to my brows.

How does addiction slash family love?
How do I possibly thrive, not just survive,
amidst generational trauma engrained
in a prairie of grief?

Dear One,
I am here to support you.
Life is tough but so are you…
Nature shows you
how to thrive in times of despair.

Evil energy and the power of love are at war.
Climb into the burrows of what is unspeakable.
Battle brutality and seize the vision of love.
Dig deep into the sodden soil.
Reveal the crown roots and mend them.

Stitch yourself back together,
and suture your family
with Faith, Mystical Hope, and Love.

Grief's Ground Takes Root

I.

Throughout the Grand Canyon,
an outcry echoes abuse, addiction,
betrayal, death, discrimination,
racism, sickness, shame,
violence, war.

Grief erupts and vibrates
across the Earth.

Ancient sequoia tree
pierced by the uproar
collapses in purple dusk.

II.

Grief,
grave dignitary
cloaked and buried,
concealed in the dark forest.

Shadow moon spreads underground
through redwood's roots
to guide grief out of Earth's darkness,

Agony rises.

III.

Forest of Grief
stands headstrong
in timberland's muddy thicket.
Earth fights to harvest Spring
from grief's roots.
Meanwhile,

Life's Concerto

IV.

I rest in my TerryHill Lane garden, surrounded by
weeping willows and November's moonlight.
My feet are icy; I am numb yet alive.

Anguish, confusion, and grief
grow in my shadow body.
My fingers cannot grasp grief
as I grapple with loss.

June delivered Paul's death; 24 years old.
July delivered Luis's death; 25 years old.
October delivered Natalie's death; 86 years old.

I sit on my teak bench
to hear the fountain's final flow.
A candelabra's flame transports me
into contemplation as I wearily catch my breath.

Autumn equinox urges me:

Transplant your sorrows
swathed in summer heat.
Summer season passed away.
Trees let go of their leaves, then
drift into windy, auburn autumn.
The seasons are here
to show you the way.
There is a path through grief–

Lightning strikes my heart.

I cry out.
My grief-body
cracks open;
rhythms of agony
release from every cell.

I grasp anguish and sorrow
with reverence
wrapped in love.
Grief guides my soul
out of my shadow realm,

through dark thickets of undergrowth
to gather life's kindling.

Heartaches' bonfire
burns all night.

Transmutation
liberates pain.

Grief's fire
rises in the phoenix of my body,
a stream opens within:

Faith, Hope and Love ascend.

Explore the Tornado's Roar

Out of the blue
a tornado blows through,

wiping out everything
that I knew to be true.

Wiped out I and Thou:
cracked open life's mysteries.

What once was true
is now blown through.

Nothing is as it seems
inside the Eye of the Storm.

The Eye pierces the veil,
pierces through the stormy sky

into my heart
where I roar *Why*?

Exploring questions
I didn't know to ask.

Blood red tears surge;
raindrops bleed through the sky.

A voice whispers:
Storms don't hurt the Sky.

Can the tornado reconstruct
The Why of the I?

Now the Eternal Eye sees
from my heart into the Storm,

urging a fresh bold perspective:
How might I see beyond this veil?

IV. The Cracked Hallelujah

Velvet Cocoon

Weave a nest beneath the weeping willow
wrap my body in a velvet blanket
wail my anguish, sorrows, and grief
weep life's despair. I long
to be embraced by God's meadow.

The Wild One

I.
I've heard there are secrets
silenced in every
body
riddles revealed through a lifetime

Never mind...
I tried and tried
what else can I do?
flying through nightmares
at twilight, I shake you

I wake your vocal cords
with a midnight shriek

Scream squeezes your throat tight
to disclose what is going on below
terror chokes your courage tonight

Calm down
I am trying to breathe you
Calm down
I need to be with you

A cry
a broken drumbeat
a shriek
we've been there before

How does a shadow get lit?
edgy bones with emotions like this
acute and clear-cut
the blade feels \ so sharp
passions pierce the heart

Never mind,
let it go
I will depart.
Leave you behind

again, and again and again
out of my mind, out of my life
back in five minutes or maybe five years

Back to sleep, I go
buried deep inside
your miracle suit
until I wake you again
whispering the music of the night

II.
Decades of decadence deserted on shelves

Wild One,
Who are you?
Why are you here?
What do you need?

Secret Selves plea freedom
screaming a heap of poems
locked in your treasure chest

Clenched jaws
grinding teeth
incarcerated emotions
held back/locked in a treasure chest
moods imprisoned in cells
resentment, rage, regret
fear, angst, distress
grief, terror, horror,
contempt and despair

Do you care?
Fire blazing in my heart
water cascades down my body
I come to breakfast naked and cold
unclothed and exposed

A song whispers in the milieu
Music of the night,

I used to live alone before I knew you
it's cold and lonely in this dark dungeon
try to sleep on a hard icy cot
endlessly awake in this frozen state
blinded in the shadow
evidently, falling off the edge

There was a time
when I let you know
what was really going on
below

Every breath we drew was for you
Why have I been cast aside?
Why do I need to be cut off?
entombed in concrete

Misty Night conceives sad shadows
makes me sleep out of boundaries
risk flows through my fingertips
there was a time when you knew
what was really going on below

I remember
when I came through the light

Now, I am submerged in this cave
and stagger through murky midnights
in an effort to save you
and your parts that are not brave

In the beginning, it was consideration
in the beginning, it was contemplation
but as time goes on; it is redemption
buried underground in this concrete cave

Decades of submersion
in the cold, glacial underground
it starts innocently: smiling, hailing, saluting
but then the greeting disregards
a small inkling of anger, disgust, deceit
Desire is expected to wait

Life's Concerto

Wait, wait, wait.

Until the state is shut
I forgot how to touch
I did my best, even though it wasn't enough
Voulez-vous coucher avec moi ce soir?

Maybe all I really
learned in this life
is the cry you hear at night
the cracked hallelujah

How does this happen again and again?
Is it too much to comprehend?
In an effort to help and to hold
we get stuck underground
and lose our chance to be bold

and witness our secret selves
Where does this life go?
How can we really know?

So much fire squelched
What is it all about?
Does any of it matter?
fire, water, air, dirt
there is a crack in my cave
dirt and water make mud
knee-deep in sludge

The wild one in the dungeon wants out

I want out

Never
Again
At last
Forever

Freed

Reclaim the Stranger Within

Sperm and egg unite,
miraculous baby grows.
Where do children come from?
Strangely, no-body really knows.

Mother and child cry out
as they voyage through birth canal.
Humankind born wounded,
bruises encircle our eyes.

We land inside a family—
generations entwined in time.
Family constellations flare:
Mother, Father, Sister, Brother,
Lover, Husband, Wife.

Inside the family constellation
secret selves estranged
and buried for generations.
Eventually, reborn in a new baby.

We clench profound questions,
not sure of anything.

Who are we?

We are destitute and divided.
Hazards beckon every day.
Compulsion, craving, obsession
devour our anguish and pain.

Underworld gravity
drags us into thick mud.
Badgers, bats, raccoons, ravens,
frogs, groundhogs, hawks, and snakes:

All creatures *other* than our secret selves.
So much confusion, so many aches.
Poisonous venom seeps out,
we are helpless, ruptured, and stunned.

We must explore profound questions,
not sure of anything or anyone.
Why are we here?

We do not understand
hence, we lash out at the exile.
Not realizing that the strangers rising
up in our own backyard are:

Secret selves estranged
and buried for generations.
We must sit in the bonfire together,
suffer through rhythms of rebirthing pains.

Explore the nature of the stranger.

What do we need?

Witness the refugees' anguish.
Embrace the stranger's cry for help:
extend a hand. Let us
hold each other tight.

Feel each other's heartbeat
until we see the light.
Become newborn again,
liberate spirit and soul.

Life's Concerto

Section V

Monastic Mother

*"Forgive yourself for not knowing
what you didn't know before you learned it."*
— Maya Angelou

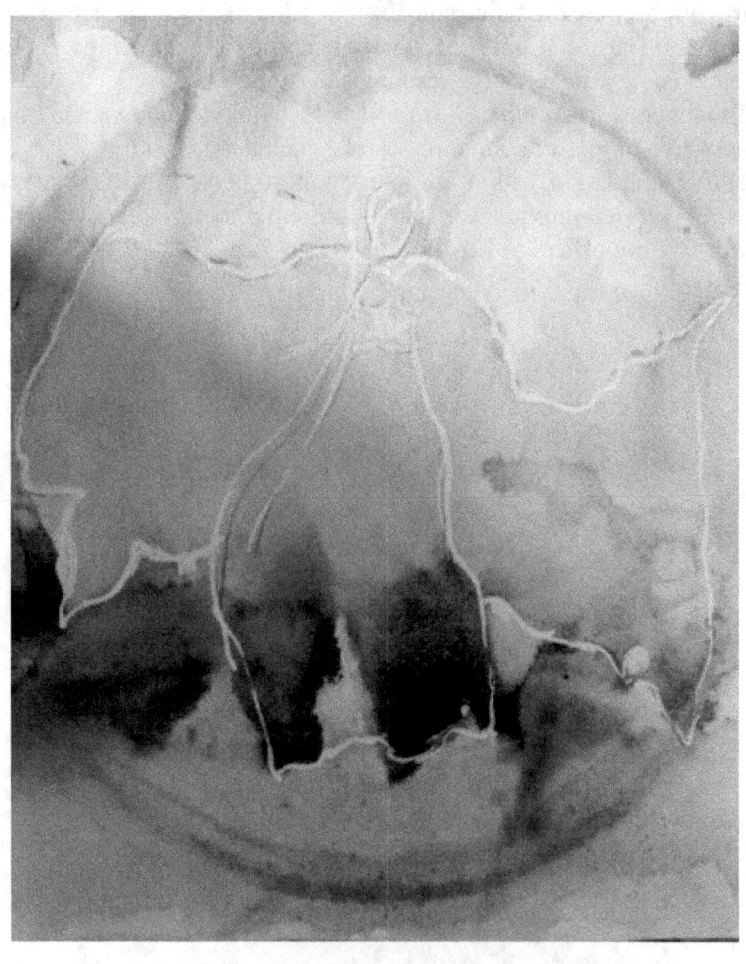

My life involves a sacred contract:

> *My job is to discover the wisdom and creativity in every individual that I encounter, to unleash the deepest purpose for living, and to evolve the human spirit.* (Goslin-Jones, 1999)

In my life, companioning and serving others is a pathway to growth. My internal monastery, combined with inner guides, offers me an opportunity to serve in ways that I could not do alone. Even though I would never seek hardship, I learn and grow from these experiences. My poems and artwork become medicine and an expression of inner guidance. Through this process, I grow in unexpected ways, and at the same time, I develop newfound energy and creative resources to support others.

The poems in *Monastic Mother* helped me to understand that the fundamentals of my individuation process include:

1) Contemplation within my internal monastery, 2) Listening to inner guides, 3) Service through harvesting and embodying creative energy, 4) The world is my office, 5) Love is my work.

Monastic Mother
(Poetry collage 2017–2021)

Mother Tree sprawling, reaching, and rooted
breathing life on Calistoga's shady porch
even when cabins were erected around
her trunk, arms, roots and branches,
Mother Tree still rooted in mud
accepts a vow of stability…

*She is the one who didn't know
but does know
surfacing from dream life
in the luminous moonlight*

Mother Tree kissed by the sun
births and embraces future creations
her veins transport water and nectar
her leaves reflect bronze and emeralds
falling and rising with the seasons
She carries her vow of stability…

*She dwelt in lightening
absorbing stormy skies and birth pains,
generating a shelter and home
for the miracle of life*

Mother Tree rises to incredible peaks
branches reach out to the heavens
limbs scratch the dusty earth
tender shade and shelter offered
as a portal of majestic source
She shoulders her vow of stability…

*She listened to toddler dreams and
cried buckets, witnessing their wounds,
praying with angelic force
loving baby souls into adulthood*

V. Monastic Mother

Mother Tree encased in dense body
her bark is living tissue transmuting energy
protecting her beloved family
her outer crust unites life's flavors
while inner life embraces mystical beauty
She welcomes her vow of stability…

She sows seeds of hope
humming underground earth prayers
for her family and the sorrows of society
while holding a mystical rose

Mother Tree shifting, swaying, yet rooted
her chandelier crown comprised of foliage
invisible buds waiting to burst open
bluebirds land and chant their ballads
to prepare a path for spirit's breath
She cherishes her vow of stability…

She reveres Mother Earth
and invokes her sacred heart,
monastic mother with a secret life
vibrating with creation

Mother Tree holds treasures in her trunk
lifetimes of stories come and go
and even though her nature is
rooted in mud; rooted in mud
her branches wave goodbye; in time
She relinquishes her vow of stability…

She stands with life's mystery
offering an invisible union,
traveling through all realms
loving into eternity

Gathering Her Wits

Mother Bluebird fled her nest.

In a flash, she crashed
into my kitchen window.

Feathers flew—
she fell to the ground,
collapsed on her belly.

Shaken
stunned
shocked.

She did not move nor shift
but gathered her wits.

An eternity passed—

Miraculously,
she collected her courage,
mobilized her wingspan.

Then,
serenely soared
into the stormy clouds.

This Too Shall Pass

Lost and now found,
desolate and now quiet,
engulfed and now settled,
traveling and now home.

I feel abandoned,
yet part of me understands.
Let go…do not stay stuck
in what could have been.

At first,
emotions consumed me.
Now, I know
this too shall pass,
through the mysterious life path.

Go deep and maybe
find space to
care for body
care for mind
care for spirit.

Embrace the mystery

Carve out periods of immersion,
precious moments in the garden.
Listen to the fountain,
water droplets bathe my brain

Tell me, soul – which way should I go?
take me on my path.

Step slowly into the wise forest
where the mystery resides.

Silent retreats have been taken away
structure fresh awareness for myself,
excavate emotions,
unravel the ground of being.

Life's Concerto

Treasure this sacred pause,
sing in the garden,
plant poetry,
listen to music of the soul.

Be still.

Mother's Vow

I.

Mother and baby voyage together,
day by day, month by month,
their bodies and souls
intertwined through pregnancy,
till birthing into life's light.

Time slips by swiftly
while whispering winds
snap a sacred bond
between mother and child.

Possessed by time's arrow,
an otherworldly Force pierces
Earth's atmosphere;
the Force digs a mysterious ravine
to a threshold door—
their souls' code rips open.

Pregnant now with distress,
mother and child descend
underground. Then, trek
into the dark cave of their souls' passage.

They travel through rugged shadowlands
and encounter
physical labor and spiritual birth.
Footsteps stumble
on inconceivable gorges.
Nightmares surface as
they tumble into the Earth,
to a place of no return—

Heartaches unearth grottos.
Both souls struggle through barren valleys,

alone yet interlaced.

Mother's heart holds broken parts.
Her bruised body wrapped in velvet blanket,
she births and nurses, loves and grieves
this raw and wounded life journey.
Amidst back pain and strain,
her broken heart
spirals into energetic chains,
that bind and jail.

II.

I never thought it was possible…
to stagger so far from each other.

By
nighttime
titanic pain
swarms through me.
In my dream, I see
my waist, hips and back
swaddled in lace gauze.
The Angelic Forces of
Intimacy, Tenderness, and Mystery
wrap and stitch me back together.
I unwrap and unwrap and unwrap
the lace gauze enveloping my body.
Presence generates a gift within my being
a spiritual threshold is delivered
I surrender and walk through the doorway.

Please dear god, hold my hand
let me breathe with my babies,
even though I do not understand.
Please dear god – embrace our souls.

III.
You are—
Earth Dancer of Change,
dancing with the vow
of mother and child's
interlaced soul's code.

Earth Dancer of Change,
you don't have to bear all life's agony.
Lay down your body of burdens.
Gently, stitch life back together.

Earth Dancer of Change,
mother and child must walk alone
and at the same time journey together
to witness and then,
transcend life's struggles.

Earth Dancer of Change,
embrace this message
between mother and child's
souls' code.
Your mother's vow
embodies wisdom to embrace
spirals of unity and love,
that descend into the ground
then ascend into the sky.

Earth Dancer of Change –
it's okay…
Release, unravel your soul's code.
let go
Breathe, breathe, breathe.

Life's Concerto

Music flows through me.
Compose fresh thresholds.
Miracles at play—

I.
I contemplate my unborn body
cocooned before birth, then
contemplate my baby body
swimming through Mother's womb.

Contemplate my birthday body
piercing the atmosphere
of Mother Earth.

I embody surging waves
of oceanic sensations
glowing with mystical warmth.

II.
My body becomes a chalice
for circadian cadence as
I ponder the deep sea of
pregnant emotions
voyaging through me.

My body ripens
into a vessel
for earth, breath, and fire.

I miraculously morph
into lover, wife, mother
and dancer of life.

Trekking around Mother Earth,
we hike, skate, spin, swim
in our saltwater body.

III.
Swept away
by life's stormy waves
my heartroom ruptures,
the grotto door to my soul opens.

In the beginning,
I slide, skid and crash on life's icy roads,
at that juncture, my sea veins twist
and turn into frozen crystals.

Glacial ice invites
me to walk on water
in my wounded miracle suit,
I learn to trailblaze.

Freezing and thawing are Nature's Way,
life pours into my heart and soul.

IV.
Dwelling in the deep-sea shadows
miraculous love and oceanic moods fuse
inside my body's music room,
the grotto door to my soul opens.

Consider the Composer
engraving life's musical notes,
consider the waves of spirit
playing music from my soul.

Each season the ocean breakers
bestow birth again and again.

Climb the mountain
bathe in the sea
frolic in the garden
float with clouds
skydive backwards
embrace Mother Earth.

Life's Concerto

The universe and I intertwine,
we surf the currents of life,
and unite in the tides of my body
dwelling in these miraculous moments.

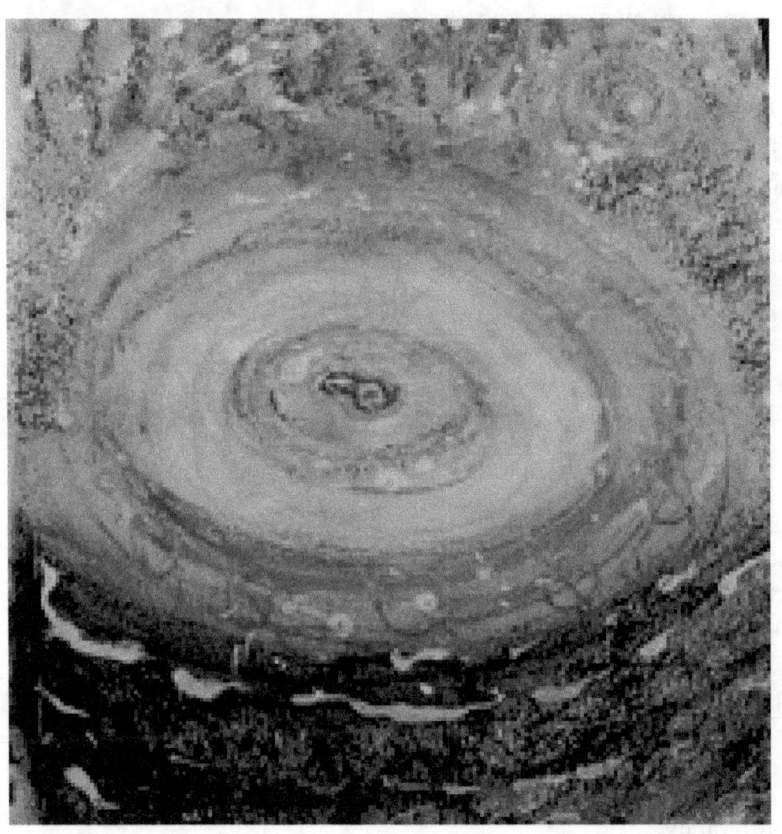

Cloud Calligraphy

Cumulous cloud veil
soars high above sapphire sky.
Spring snowstorm awakens Earth,
as fiery air and water merge.

I sit and wait with my mother
in her final hours of life.
We ponder Nature's transitions
and gaze out the window
at the mysterious spring, snow clouds.

A cloud unravels and cracks open.

What if sky clouds transmit
telegraphs of spirit's geography?

Clouds float and dissolve
in the same way ice melts,
and cascades into a waterfall.
Clouds teach us how to
be fluid and flow.

Heaven and Earth merge,
as does our body and soul.

What if
cloud calligraphy
comprises secret messages
ascending from Earth's soul?

In this moment…
I hold her hand
and witness my mother
step over the edge,
to grasp the miracle.

As above,
so below…

Life's Concerto

Thanksgiving Table

When I awaken
to plan our Thanksgiving feast,
I find myself lackluster,
an ashen cloud.

Tending daily life and serving as
handmaiden exhausts me.
My soul hidden, my inner
self out of sync.
Chatter bruises my being.

I long to sit with my family and sob together,
pour out buckets of spirit-rain,
unravel this earthly life puzzle.

My desire is to create our family circle,
shelter underneath a divine velvet blanket
interlaced with mystical hope and love,
embroidered with truth and transformation.

I thirst for purpose, passion, and spirit.

Yet, my craving for depth drowns others,
I close my floodgates and shift my rhythm.
I wade into shallow waters to seek a normal flow,
but *normal* is painfully absent.
My body surges with clashing signals.

To survive, I enter my mystery room,
my secret, ethereal dwelling place
within my soul-body.

I carry grief kindling
to burn in my heart cave,
family logs roar.
I pour my sorrow into
a baptismal pool.

Life's Concerto

I invite guidance:

Dear Wise Elder,
Please, help me —
to shower others with love,
even though I am washed out.

I will rise out of this bed.
I will trudge to the grocery store.
I will cook turkey, stuffing,
sweet potatoes, green bean casserole,
and pumpkin pie, even though
this food does not nourish me.
Wearing emotional armor,
I will plunge into the holiday.

Alone, I journey
into a jungle of entangled family trees.
As I float over the dining table,
I hear my Wise One offer a blessing:

May our ancestors' gaping wounds
be showered with love.
May underground generational trauma
surface for healing.
May our jungle of family tree entanglements,
be transformed with love's light.
May we cultivate and nurture,
our heavenly garden while still on Earth.
May there be a seat,
at our Thanksgiving table,
for each family member's soul,
May we awake before we die.

NorthStar Cherry Season

I.
Grandma Marion
visited my dreamlife last night.

A crystal bowl of Michigan NorthStar cherries
lingered on her kitchen table.

Grandma brewed jasmine blossoms,
and poured green tea
into her fine China.

Sipping warm tea, we witnessed a goldfinch
and cardinal greet each other
at the backyard birdfeeder.

As a teenager, I spent summers
working with my grandparents in *Marion's Rock Shop*.
Grandma designed jewelry and
repaired antique dolls. One of the rooms in her shop
was named "Doll Hospital."

Mornings, Grandpa Hull, dressed in a blue jean shirt
and a turquoise bolo tie tended the garden
while cooking our luncheon of baked chicken and acorn squash.
Afternoons, he cut and polished stones unearthed
from the Great Lakes and winter rock hunts in Tucson.

Grandma transformed Petoskey stones, jasper,
tiger eye, and turquoise into exquisite jewelry.
I sold their merchandise to quirky artists and musicians
who trekked two miles from the Interlochen Arts Academy.
I was envious of these poets, painters, and violin players
clothed in navy blue corduroy knickers.

II.
Grandma read my tea leaves.
I eagerly awaited this closing ritual
that we shared after each meal.

Grandma's tea leaves revealed riddles of life.
As I listened to her tea leaf reading,
a cyclone surged from my heart,
rising to my brow.

I traveled down a dusty path
and crossed through an archway
into the NorthStar cherry grove.

I asked Grandma,
What is the taste and spirit
that you are passing onto me?
What are you saying?
Can you tell me clearly?

Grandma was an alchemist
creating pies straight from NorthStar cherry trees.
She said,
We must harvest cherries and bake pastries.
NorthStar cherries are tart and glisten like rubies.
Cherry season bears fruit in summer's extreme heat.
Cherries are laced with fleeting time—
they bruise easily, yet
cherries invite us to
taste life's bittersweetness.
Harvest grace
from each
juicy
moment.

Grandma's spirit blew across my shoulder blades as
she crossed over an invisible threshold.

Magnolia Family Tree

Mystic, monk, shaman, sage…
caretaker of silence
guardian of daylight and radiant night
a traveler through all realms.

Monastic Magnolia roots freely,
hums underground prayers
for Earth family.
Prays in place
for eternity.

Monastic Magnolia vibrates with Creation.
Embraces what the Earth naturally bestows:
rain, wind, blessings from the sky.

Absorbs birth pains from stormy skies'
moans and cries, sometimes sighs.
Surrounded by Earth's sorrows
and steeped in a secret life.
Asking for nothing.

Monastic Magnolia stands,
rooted in life's mystery.
Bequeaths an invisible union.

Loves into eternity.

Section VI

Gardener of the Soul

*"And don't think the garden loses its ecstasy in winter.
It's quiet, but the roots are down there riotous."*
—Rumi

Immersion in a garden is an encounter with each changing season and serves as a pathway toward personal transformation. We are intertwined and entangled with Nature. Each season, there is growth *and* struggle in my garden. There is tremendous letting go that transmutes into a new birth. For as long as I can remember, I have tended a garden. My garden reveals the shifts of each season and mirrors the changes occurring across my lifetime.

I have planted and nurtured hundreds of flowers, bushes, and trees. I am spellbound as I listen to the birds' powerful music sung alongside the trees, flowers, and wind. I hear layers and layers of musical notes each season. Winter is a time of dormancy, yet at the same time the roots travel and grow in their underground community. Springtime births lime green sprouts and white magnolia buds. Summer heat blazes and the canna lilies leap to six feet tall. Fall is the ultimate time for letting go. Leaves plunge to the ground. I feel a huge shift in autumn, and it feels like everything is dying.

Every autumn, I revisit the realization that "Yes, we are going to die. We die again and again as we cross the threshold into new seasons of life." We travel through our lifecycle as infants, children, teenagers, into young adulthood and midlife, and if we live long enough, there may be the gift of becoming a wise elder. Within each of these small deaths resides an opportunity for rebirth.

Gardener of the Soul asks, "Why wait so long to experience miracles when they exist every day in our very own backyards?" Each day brings a metaphorical garden to walk through as we experience our sorrows, our despair, and our joy. We co-create with Nature and the creatures in our backyard. Through this process, we simultaneously live a human and divine experience. The poems in this section are about humanity and the divine working together to manifest miracles and to birth our creative potential on Earth. Together, may we tend our garden and honor each season of our life.

Our TerryHill Lane Garden

I. Winter

A white fluffy bedspread
shelters our winter garden,
Mourning doves coo on a frosty branch.
Larks warble, crows caw, starlings whistle.

In the early winter dawn
robins chirp and perch
upon the freezing purple leaves
of Little Flirt Nandina.

Starlings join the robins,
and patiently anticipate
a breakfast offering:
gourmet sunflower seeds
served banquet style.

Meanwhile, buried beneath
a soft snowy blanket,
saffron crocus sleep close by,
first to awake on Valentine's Day.

II. Spring

A March storm brews,
waterdrops stream from the sky,
thunder vibrates, the garden quivers.

Garden squabbles erupt amongst
a backyard bird colony:
Bully blue jays collide with the sparrows.
Cardinals pray for peace.

I plant lavender and basil,
for Earth Day.
The garden creatures
dream of a fragrant future.
Crystal raindrops sow seeds of hope.

III.   Summer

In June, our feathered creatures
warble in many dialects
proclaiming their summer passion.

Baby Robin is birthed and loved,
snuggling into Willow's springtime nest.
Weeping Willow bends down
to stroke the ground. Dewdrops stream
from Willow's lacy leaves.

The summer heat blazes,
canna lilies leap to six feet tall,
while elephant ears dance and
create music with their colossal leaves.

Bluebirds calm the summer garden,
whistling ballads beside the
owls who hoot sunset lullabies.

IV.   Autumn

Garden temperatures plunge,
tree branches drop their leaves.
High in the sky, the barren branches
script mystical messages for all to read.

It is time to take flight—

Mallard ducks, starlings, blackbirds, and geese
croon a plea to pack up.
Leave the Missouri nest at daybreak,
fly high, cross borders, and migrate south.
As I walk outside to say goodbye,
leaves crunch under my feet.

I recline on the splintered teak bench.
The wind hums with a low-pitched chill
while the birds nestle into the bamboo.
The warblers harmonize and sing a goodbye lullaby.

Life's Concerto

Why wait for heaven when the
Garden of Eden
resides in our backyard.

Gardener of the Soul

Innermost poet
gardener of the soul
dreadlocks drape her breasts.
Gusty wind breathes her essence,
as she shifts and sways with the storm.

Innermost poet
gardener of the soul,
was born knowing that
humanity's apple orchards
need thunderstorms to flourish.

Owl Medicine

Owl's enchanting eyes
transmit a wisdom voyage
trust the twisted limb

Cicadas Line Dance

The Earth cracks open
to liberate cicadas
from 17 years of sleep.

Adorned for mating season
they burst with passion.

Longing for soul mates
crowds of cicadas line dance
on our cherry tree.

Nature's Secret Messages

Dear Ones,

We are a dust speck
traversing the universe
looking for our soul

dark, weary sadness
stitched into our aching heart
bound in mystery

shattered heart and soul
engage divine dialect
to repair lifeforce

charism of tears
poetic soul messages
jewels of emotions

stark branches waiting
tiny invisible buds
prepare freedom's path

gliding through garden
monarch butterflies migrate
feasting on milkweed

full moon at midnight
frog chorus calls beloved
to bathe in fountain

surrender this path
listen to flowing waters
it is time to plunge

Life on the Web

A quarter past sunset, moon's shadow plunges
and illuminates the garden village.

Spider's workstation lights up to reveal
gauze tightropes linking the hydrangea trees.

A firefly lands, spellbound
in the cone flower's pocket.

It takes weeks for the spider,
to build bridges and string nightlights.

Sculpted inside spider's web—
resides a secret path with a message.

*There is always a place to crossover
and design webs of harmony.*

Firefly's mining headlights pave a pathway
within the deep eclipse.

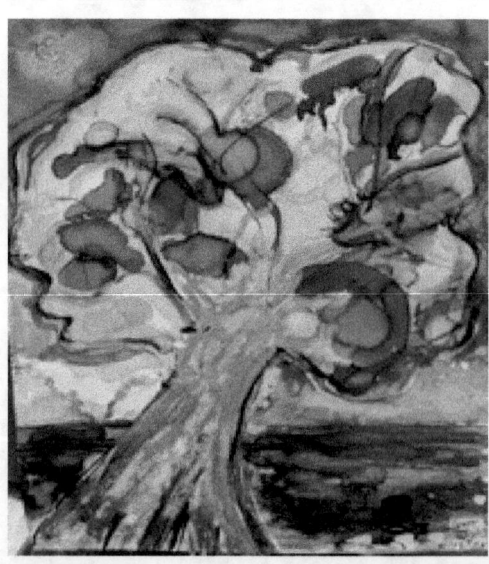

Tree Spirit Summons

Up high in garden's giant oak tree
awaiting my call,
Tree Spirit awakens.

Show me something, Tree Spirit.
How do I harvest your secret messages?
Autumn Garden converses among
pink clouds, burning bushes, brilliant red maples.

Redbud trees turn yellow.
Their golden leaves toasted
in solar and lunar rays
tumble and windsurf:
falling, flying, floating.

It is here: time clock harkens.
It is here: Autumn reminds me,
leaves fall every season.

Asters wait all year, blooming in autumn
expressing their momentous dance.
You would not think that each flower
would have to dance and bloom every day of the year.

Garden blooms, garden rests,
garden goes dormant.
Garden roots are wild down there,
seeking creative nourishment.

Tree Spirit, I have never held
rainwater in my hands.
I have tried, but it seeps through gaps.
Rainwater cascades at its own pace:

fountain of youth
fountain of life
fountain of wisdom
flows through life

emerging at its own pace
hour by hour
day by day
decade by decade.

Up high in garden's giant oak tree,
Tree Spirit awaits
my acceptance of the invitation.
Tree Spirit, I am listening,
I hear your secret message:

Love this stage, love this depth,
love the surging power
emerging from your soaring spirit—
pioneer into ethereal spirit realms.

Born From the Heavens

Guided by our ancient mother and father
I voyaged to Earth
as a Modern-Day Pilgrim.

I tread from Saint Louis to Big Sur
to hang out on a limb
and trek amongst oceans of brain waves
before I dive and swim with marine life.

With my husband and sons
I jump from the Missouri plains of the ordinary
and leap out of a Cessna plane
to skydive into the extraordinary.

As a Modern-Day Pilgrim,
I crisscross thresholds
and search with a miner's light
for the shadow and gold deep within.

I excavate medial ground
and discern life through
mandorlas and Tibetan sounds
then climb Machu Picchu with my son
to connect my soul to the earth.

I leave the known at home
to step into the wild and sacred
mystery of life and
travel as a Modern Day Pilgrim.

Dawn's Chorus

*"The Sea is a musical composition
that yearns to be heard."*

Sunrise and ocean waves
awaken Seabrook's wildlife
as I emerge from dreamland.

Dawn's song echoes beyond the shoreline;
my rubber soles click softly along the wooden boardwalk.
A breeze caresses my forehead.

Cardinals skim saltwater collected
in sweetgrass during last night's high tide.
Ocean mist rises from the dew.

Red winged blackbirds launch into a trill,
synchronizing each syllable while
sparrows sing soprano.

Earth's bird symphony is a sweet alarm clock.
Awakening the seagulls and brown pelicans
while hushing the deer and bobcats back to sleep.

Piping Plovers and Red Knots migrate thousands of miles,
flying through storms to seek calm refuge here,
led by instinct, starry nights, and family bonds.

Each morning yearns to be heard,
and I long to witness Nature's symphony.

My body aches for Seabrook's Ocean.

When I imagine my departure,
I miss the creatures that sleep and awaken
on each side of the boardwalk.

Life's Concerto

They inspire my liberation.
In this moment,
>Stand Still
>Close my eyes
>Empty my mind…

Symphony of birds sing to me.
>I can't get enough
>I can't get enough
>I can't get enough

I become the sea.

Section VII

Miracles at Play

What if we surrender, cross over, and discover a doorway into a new way of being?

This section, *Miracles at Play* was written across my lifespan from age 17 years old to the current day. A *miracle* is an astonishing and desirable event that natural or scientific laws cannot explain. Some people consider a miracle to be a divine phenomenon that is experienced within human life. In the context of these poems, the term *play* enjoys a double meaning.

Miracles at Play comprises synchronicity. *Miracles at Play* engages qualities of silence and presence while inviting spontaneity and improvisation into daily living. I experience my body as a spiritual and musical instrument that embodies divine energy. I play with Nature and listen to the musical notes that arise in my life. Each season generates new compositions. This initiates a deeper listening to my inner nature and new music arises for my *Life's Concerto*. Ultimately, I will leave this cherished instrument behind and *Free Solo with the Universe*.

Stunned with Grace

I take a pew on the teak bench
beneath the crepe myrtle tree.

My body becomes a vessel
to grasp creation.

My hands caress silky bark—
language travels to my fingertips.

Branches become ablaze with white light,
cone-shaped blossoms explode
like Roman candles.

Everything is possible.

Silence is the Portal to my Soul

Gently, I unravel papyrus
to decipher a message. Calligraphy
marks each ashen page on the embossed scroll.
Ancient passages disclose a book of maps,
a secret dialect.

A candle ignites as I meditate and cross
into an entrance of stillness. Silence drips
onto each ashen page and illuminates
the darkness.

Hear the hush—

A transparent message is engraved
on the page. I touch the drops of silence
with stillness and witness
the ancient scroll of my soul.

My soul bestows a silent
passageway through my heart.

I dwell
in the doorway of eternity.

Hear the sacred hush—

Mississippi River's Sunrise Surprise

I gaze into the Mississippi shoreline,
as daybreak paints with sunlight.

Brushstrokes of pink and orange
stream across crimson clouds.

A hazy heart emerges
on sky's holy canvas.

Sunrise surprise whispers,
Love is your work.

Miracles at Play

An orphan to my Earth parents,
A mom to my 30-something sons.
A daughter of 60-plus years to the Earth.
A wife to my beloved husband of 40 years.

An ensemble of musicians and a choir
inhabit my inner chambers.
It is a blessing to sing the many ages
of my life's chorus.

Really—how old am I?

When I was 11, I imagined falling in love
with a brown-eyed man,
that had dark hair and a hairy chest.
I wrote about him in my diary.

It took patience and many years
until finally, I met him
at a dinner meeting —my first job
at Blackburn College in Student Affairs.

Forever—I remember my first glimpse.
This dark-haired man with a beard
and a *Rolling Rock* shirt, ordering dinner
at the Glades restaurant in Carlinville, Illinois.
I asked my colleague who he was,
"An engineer from Monterey."

My mystical guide spoke in my mind,
"This is the man you wrote about in your diary,
when you were 11."

Really—how old am I?

We sit on wooden steps that link
Seabrook's shoreline to the Atlantic Ocean.
The beach path hidden under the evening tide.
Waves crash high and dampen our feet.

Life's Concerto

Time passed so fast…
My husband's dark hair,
transformed to silvery white
Sitting on Seabrook Island's dock,
we embark upon a fresh era in life.

The August moon rises from the Ocean Tide,
a kaleidoscope of sea sound
chants to us….and advises us to
pause for these – miraculous moments.

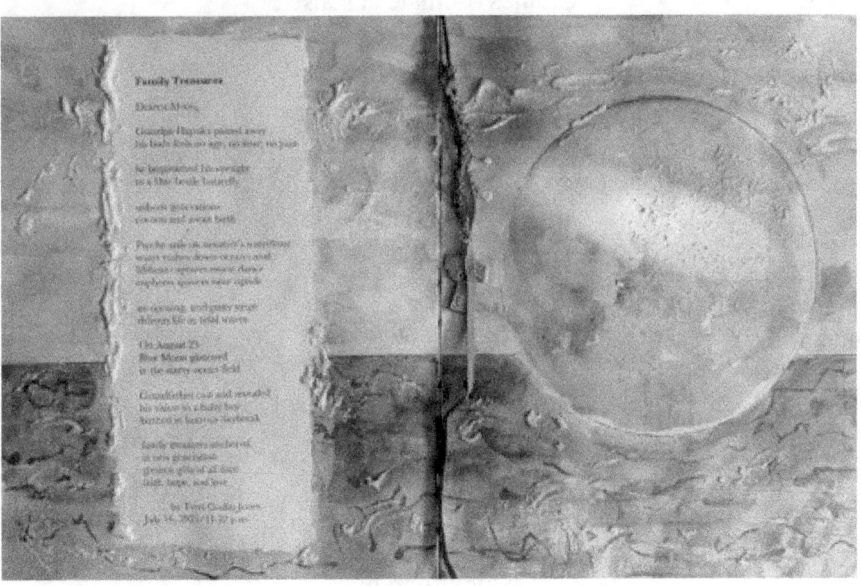

Universal Circle

Look up to see
a gateway,
an opening for
all to *be*

A Universe within a universe—

Chimes oscillate at sunset.
My eyes open
like Enso circles
to the mysterious cosmos

Constellations connect the dots,
from our eyes, to our ears
to our heart

Stand Still
What do you hear?
Thunder-rolling waves-midnight skies
like an unbounded ocean
overflowing with
galactic life

Sky's shoreline
breaks open.
Silence saturates darkness
with luminous stillness

Our bodies
a spiritual masterpiece vibrating
inside life's labyrinth

Healing fields
of hope surface

Medicine of the universe.

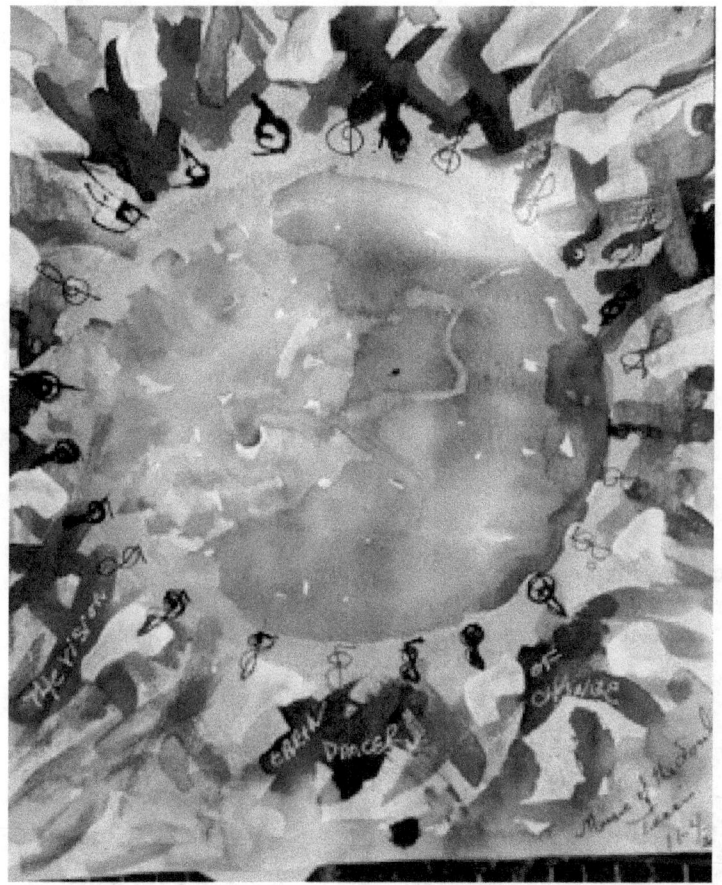

My Moon's Embrace

At midnight, I crack open
my bedroom window
and invite the moon inside,
to breathe with me.

The moon climbs up the trellis,
glides through my balcony window
tenderly touches my toes and fingertips.

Enveloping my whole being
with its shimmering light.

Spirit flows through my body.

Lost in Medical Measures

The DEXA scan breaks my body,
into elemental pieces
to measure a fracture risk.

When it comes to assessing my body,
the sum of my bones
is lost in a medical paradigm.

My backbone appraised as deficient.
Apparently, osteoporosis invaded my skeleton.

Reduced to parts of a whole.
Is the calculation worth it?
Are there solutions to the equation?

I do not want to be a crooked elder,
who cannot look people in the eye.

They say, if I ride a horse
or surf on a board,
I might fall and fracture.

Yet, adventure is essential,
to stay alert and alive....

Why spend all this time
on all these medical tests,
for what purpose?

Why not opt out of the medical system,
STOP the "evaluations"?
Is the calculation worth it?
Are there solutions to the equation?

Forgo, a phase of captivity,
my body handcuffed,
detained and confined,
like a hostage.

Instead, why not,
seize this final chapter,
as a free person...
free of evaluation,
free of opinion,
free of diagnosis.

Flow with the seasons
Fall from the vine —
perish when it is time.

Does it matter
if I teeter cautiously,
or is it best to breathe boldly?

Why can't I—
adjust and accept,
micro breakdowns
and shifts inside my body?

We are greater,
than the sum
of our parts.

We are whole.
We are holy.

Dear Body

Here we are at life's supper hour.
The clock will soon strike midnight,
and our time together is fleeting.

During this life journey,
you blessed me with your *Miracle Suit,*
and clothed my soul
with tenderness and strength.

We loved, we birthed, we sobbed.
We savored, we saw, we breathed.
We listened, we grew, we ran.
We stood on our head, we swam,
We scratched the surface, we dug deep.
We wept with weeping willows.
We sang, we planted, we painted.
We wrote, we slept, we skydived.
We dreamt.
We awoke.
We let go…

During all these years…

Somehow, I denied that you would
depart and disconnect from my *Self.*
We have been so intertwined —
like bark on the trunk of a tree,
I did not see you as distinct.

In these final days,
I vow to listen with compassion to
your messages, your whispers, your sighs,
your cravings, your yearnings,
the touch of your skin,
the vistas that arise from your eyes.

Your heart gifted me
with countless doorways
into rapture and mystery.

You, my dear *Miracle Suit* —
transported me through life.
Together, we birthed creative spirit.

When you relinquish life,
and become dust again,
please know that your mystical force
will forever reside in my soul.

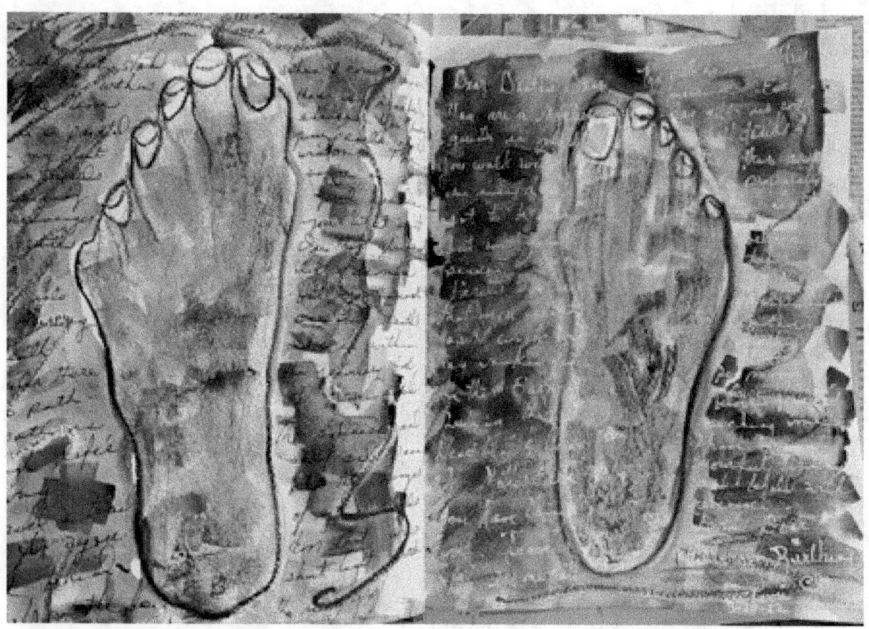

Here Am I

On this one little spot
in this one little place

years go by…
but here am I
in this same place

years go by…

time has changed
but I remain the same
and here am I

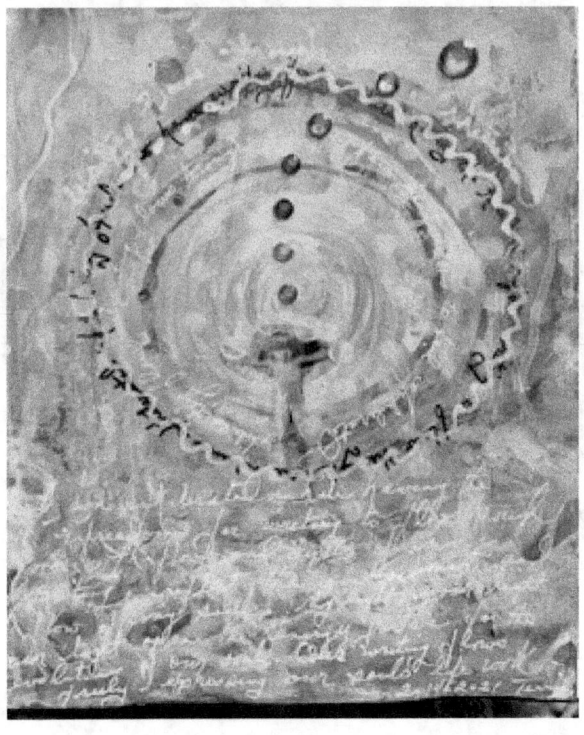

Note: This poem was written in 1974 when I was a teenager.

Free Solo

We are
a speck of dust
and yet we
traverse
the universe

LOVE...
so delighted....

Letter to Reader

Dear Reader,

Life's Concerto is a process of artistic inquiry that I hope will be helpful to you. I have learned that contemplation through art guides me into an internal monastery where I seek guidance. Poetry is a form of artmaking that helps me open doors to healing and embrace hope for the complexities in life. This book is about the seasons of life, including childhood, mid-life, marriage, being a parent, family member, teacher, and universal sojourner.

The poems were written and revised over many years. As I re-read them, I recognize that a poem reflects a portion of an experience and yet it might be interpreted by the reader as the totality of that encounter. But life itself is in flow, and we are changing moment by moment.

Life is saturated with challenges and struggles, and at the same time, life overflows with love. Please reach out with any feedback and poetry you want to share. I would enjoy hearing from you and can be reached via my website: www.terrigoslin-jones.com.

As our journey continues,

May we be open to our higher spiritual powers,
May we be infused with an open heart and receive love,
May we understand the consequences of our actions,
May we seek reconciliation,
May we help other struggling souls,
May we be a force of love and strength,
May we shift our planetary consciousness,
May we greet blessings of transformation,
May we grow as a universal family,
May we breathe in mystical hope,
May we breathe out mystical love.

Love is Our Work,

Terri Goslin-Jones, PhD

Addendum A

This section offers poetry invitations to stimulate your imagination. You are encouraged to play with these ideas in an expressive arts journal as a process to launch your creative process. Your journal is a private place to freely express yourself with words, colors, images, collages, and poetry. Poems and images will emerge, and you can develop your writing into your personal poetry collection.

Some of the invitations may unlock psychological doors that are startling or overwhelming, especially if there is a history of trauma. The creative process connects us to our emotional and sensory awareness and, at the same time, opens us to our healing and integrative potential. There may be times when you choose to share your poetry with a trusted counselor/therapist or supportive friend. As discussed in the Introduction, there are benefits to reading your poetry out loud and to creating and writing in a community.

Personally, I have participated in a Creative Spirit Circle since 2011 with five other members (Goslin-Jones, et al., 2023) and a poetry triad since 2020. I am also in a monthly writing group and attend or lead frequent expressive arts workshops. My community helps me cultivate and maintain a healthy creative practice.

Expressing your poetic voice can be fortified with a ritual that prepares your mind, body, and spirit. The timing for this ritual can vary from five minutes to hours of creative play. When your time is limited, set a timer and know that you can return later.

A Creative Ritual

"When you do things from your soul, you feel a river moving in you, a Joy."
— *Rumi*

1. Light a candle.
2. Read a short inspirational quote or poem. Or select a word or phrase as an affirmation.
3. Connect to the wisdom of your body with a few minutes of silence.
4. As a warm-up, begin by using your non-dominant hand to draw colors and images before you respond in writing.

5. Experiment by selecting a question below, then respond intuitively with colors, images, or a collage. Spontaneously layer words or phrases on top.
6. Use your art journal page as a launching pad to write a poem or prose.
7. Close your creative session with gratitude and a promise to return.

Poetry Invitations

"You must not be afraid of playing wrong notes. Just forget it, play it wrong! But play!" —Alan Watts

Section I
What Sides of Myself Need to Be Heard?
"When you listen with your soul, you come into rhythm and unity with the music of the Universe." —John O' Donohue

1. Ask the question, "What sides of myself need to be heard"? Invite your lost or secret selves out of hiding. Sit in silence for 10 minutes. Be open to all images that surface. Use your question as a line or title to launch your poem. Describe what emerged from your secret selves.
2. What musical instrument would you like to play that has been buried in your closet? Write about the sounds, notes, song, and message.
3. Who lives in your inner neighborhood? Describe the characters. Use details: clothes, hair, personalities, names, voices, childhood memories. Invite the characters to cross over time thresholds to dialogue with each other.
4. What is defrosting in your neighborhood's freezer? How can you use these ingredients in your life?
5. Take a drink of water. Describe how you quench your thirst.
6. Write a letter from your Mystical Guide or a Wise Elder.

Section II
Tidal Waves
"If you realize you are the ocean, you will never be afraid of the waves. If you forget this, you will get seasick every day. Bring loving presence to the waves." —Tara Brach

Life's Concerto

7. Look out your window and describe your landscape. Use color, scent, shapes, textures, sounds. Use your fingers and arms as a picture frame. What do you see when you reduce and widen your view?
8. Travel to your interior realm. Sit quietly for five minutes. Describe your interior landscape. What is a metaphor(s) for what you see or feel? For five minutes, write without censoring. Use sounds, colors, shapes, scents, textures.
9. In your mind's eye, open a door that has been locked within your inner landscape. What is happening? Describe what you see, hear and feel.
10. Select a force in Nature that has a message for you. (Ex. Tree, Water, Wind, Sun, Moon, Stars, Dirt, Mud). Describe this force of Nature in your poem and write notes about the emerging message and insight.
11. Write about an encounter with an animal. Describe the animal, the event, your interaction and the communication.
12. The landscape inside and outside of us constantly evolves and changes. Walk outside after a storm; fully engage your senses and notice how you are guided and protected during storms. What waves of change are evolving in your environment and in your life?

Section III
Time to Turn: Ancient Monastery
"What the caterpillar calls the end of the world, the master calls a butterfly."—Richard Bach

13. Write down 10 words that describe how you feel in your body *at this moment*. Next, use movement, music or dance to shift and integrate your body's dynamic energy. Write down 10 words or phrases *that describe your body after the music and movement*. Experiment with using your phrases/words in a poem.
14. Read the street signs in your inner neighborhood. What names and pictures are on the signs?
15. Take a mindful walk through a labyrinth (this could be in your neighborhood or in your mind's eye) to dialogue with your life's mysteries. What melody and rhythm do you hear? Where does the path take you?

16. Turn all the lights out and view the shadows that surround you. What do you notice? What question or message is within the shadow?
17. Cross a time threshold into your dream life. This could be a nightdream or a daydream. Record your experience. What do you see? Who do you meet? What are you doing? What do you learn?
18. Investigate time in your poem by adding a stanza(s) such as: As we speak, Days gone by, Eventually, Just this minute, Lately, Long ago, Once upon a time, Way far away.

Section IV
The Cracked Hallelujah
"There is no greater agony than bearing an untold story inside you."
—Maya Angelou

19. Write about something broken in your life (e.g., bone, dream, friendship, heart, object, promise, rule, vessel).
20. Ask the birds, "How do you know when it is time to migrate?" Ask the trees, "How do you know when to let go of their leaves?" Ask the bears, "How do you know when to hibernate?" and ask yourself, "What do I need to let go of?" Write prose or a poem with stanzas responding to each question.
21. Compose a poem or prose about a time when you have, as Frances Weller noted, *"Been brought to your knees, lived close to the ground, with the gravity of sorrow felt deep in your bones."*
22. What does your *Wild One* look like, sound like, move and feel like? How would you characterize the form and energy of your *Wild One*? What does your *Wild One* desire? What wisdom is your *Wild One* seeking to convey?
23. Who are some of the "*Strangers*" that live in your neighborhood? Transcribe a dialogue that includes your questions, conflicts, and hopes for the future. Add a stanza that starts with: Perhaps, I don't know, I hope, I wonder, or What if?
24. Write a poem as if it is a painting. Splash colors, shapes, shadows and images on your page.

Section V
Monastic Mother
"Help us to be ever faithful gardeners of the spirit, who know that without darkness nothing comes to birth, and without light nothing flowers." —May Sarton

25. Examine one of your roles within your family heritage: child, sibling, parent, spouse, partner, or grandparent. Write about a person, place, time, key event, celebration, or an episode of misfortune within this role. Piece the lines together. The poem *Monastic Mother* (2017–2021) offers an example.
26. Write about a holiday gathering, including the food, people, customs, and music of your traditions.
27. Compose a blessing or letter to an ancestor or friend. Incorporate objects from the person's life.
28. Reflect on the metaphorical and literal music of your life. Write a playlist. Select lines from songs. String them together and revise them into a poem that reflects the music of your life.
29. Write a poem about birth. This might include childbirth, labor, witnessing a birth or birthing a new part of yourself.
30. Go outside to experience a sunrise or sunset with Mother Nature—*Taste, Touch,* and *Heed* Nature. What is rising or setting in your life? Invite language to flow to your fingertips.
31. Consider ways that Mother Nature embraces you. Write a Postcard or love note to or from Mother Nature.

Section VI
Gardener of the Soul
"Across the morning sky, all the birds are leaving. How can they know that it's time to go?" — Nina Simone

32. Take a blanket, pen, and paper and lie outside on the ground. Listen, stare at the sky, and feel the ground beneath you. Transcribe the details of your experience. What messages lie underground and between the lines that you wrote down? What else did you hear but have not said?
33. Sit with a favorite tree and inquire: What roots you to grounded living? Where are your roots traveling? What nourishment do you need? How do you survive and thrive through each season? What gifts do you both bring to your community?
34. What resides in the crevices and cracks within the habitat of your life?
35. Eat an apple or cucumber. Experience this as a gift from the Earth: Notice the crunch, tang, textures, fragrance. Compose a three-line haiku with 17 syllables.

36. Walk outdoors to discover what is dying or thriving in your environment. Talk or text a message into your phone about the experience and transcribe this into a poem.
37. Contemplate what may be dormant in your environment and in your life. What wild roots are underground? What do they need to grow and re-emerge for the vibrant spring?
38. Write a poem from the perspective of a bird or animal that frequents your home. Do some research on this creature and then engage your imagination as if you could see through their eyes and body. How might it see your life? What does it know, see, or experience that is beyond your knowing?

Section VII
Miracles at Play
"Close the language door, open the love window." —Rumi

39. Select a favorite art form and write an *ekphrastic* poem. Immerse yourself in the experience by meditating with the painting, photo, drawing, sculpture, dance, or music. Write about the details of the images and your experience of the art form. Weave together the imagery and the insights you experienced, including descriptions of the art form, your experience, and insights. The poem and painting *Whispering Wind* offer an example.
40. Travel in your mind's eye to the quietest place in the universe. Taste Silence. Use all your senses, including your sixth sense, to describe your experience.
41. When you close your language door, what do you hear within the layers of boundless silence?
42. Write a letter to your body or transcribe a letter from your body. You might start with a question such as, "Dear Body, How do you feel when we consider stepping off the fast track?" or "What do we need in this new chapter of our life?"
43. Draw an Enso Circle. What thrives within your circle? What dwells outside your circle? The poem *Universal Circle* offers an example.
44. Miracles at Play: What miracle(s) crossed your path today? This could be your body/breath/vision, someone in your life, Nature, or something that brought you joy, amazement, or wonder. Describe your experience.

Addendum B: Poetry Resources

Poetry Books that have influenced my life and artistic expression.

Abimbola, K. (2022). *Saltwater demands a psalm.* Graywolf Press.
Ada, L. (2018). *The carrying poems.* Milkweed Editions.
Alexander, K. (2023). *Why fathers cry at night.* Little Brown Company.
Amidi, B. (2021). *The carousel of life: 40 Tales through poetry and art.* Bahereh.
Angelou, M. (2015). *The complete poetry.* Random House.
Bark, C. (2011). *Rumi: The big red book: The great masterpiece celebrating love and friendship.* HarperOne.
Barks, C. (2006). *A year with Rumi.* HarperCollins.
Barrett, C. (2024). *Reading wind.* Poetry Box.
Bartleson, L. (2021). *In*som*ni*a: A middle-of-the-night haibun collection.*
Bernhardt, M. (2021). *Voices of the grieving heart.* Cypress Point Press.
Blasing, R., & Konuk, M. (Eds.). (2002). *Poems of Nazim Hikmet.* Persea Books.
Bly, R. (Ed.). (1999). *The soul is here for its own joy: Sacred poems from many cultures.* Ecco Publisher.
Bly, R. Hillman, J., & Meade, M. (Eds.). (1992). *The Rag and bone shop of the heart: Poems for men.* HarperCollins Publisher Inc.
Brehm, J. (2021). *The dharma of poetry.* Wisdom Publishers.
Brehm, J. (Ed.). (2024). *The poetry of grief, gratitude and reverence.* Wisdom Publications.
Brown, J. (2019). *The tradition.* Copper Canyon Press.
Campo, R. (2018). *Comfort measures only.* Duke University Press.
Carroll, R. (2009). *Amazing change: Poetry of healing and transformation. The wisdom that illness, death, and dying provide.* Bombshelter Press.
Centolella, T. (1990). *Terra firma.* Copper Canyon Press.
Chang, V. (2021). *Dear memory: Writing on letters, silence and grief.* Milkweed Editions.
Chavis, G. (2011). *Poetry and story therapy: The healing power of creative expression.* Jessica Kingsley Publications.
Ching-Chao Li. (1984). *Plum blossom: Poems of Li Ch'Ing-Chao* (J. Cryer, Trans.). Carolina Wren Press.
Colburn, N. (2023). *I say the sky.* The University Press of Kentucky.
Cole-Dei, P., & Wilson, R. (Ed.). (2023). *Poetry of presence II: More mindfulness Poems.* Grayson Books.
Conner, J. (2008). *Writing down your soul.* Conari Press.
Davidson, M. (Ed.). (2008). *George Oppen: New collected poems.* New Directions.

Donegan, P. (2008). *Haiku mind: 108 poems to cultivate awareness and open your heart.* Shambhala Publications, Inc.
Drury, J. (1991/2006). *Creating poetry.* Writer's Digest Books.
Dumitru, C. (2003). *Listening to light.* River Lily Press.
Dumitru, C. (2019). *Elder moon.* Finishing Line Press.
Dungy, C. (2024). *Soil: The story of a black mother's garden.* Simon and Schuster.
Elliot, T.S. (1944, 2019). *Four quartets.* Faber and Faber.
Elytis, O. (2005). *Odysseus Elytis: Selected poems 1940–1979.* Anvil Press Poetry.
Fox, J. (1997). *Poetic medicine: The healing art of poem-making.* Tarcher-Putnam.
Fox, J. (1995). *Finding what you didn't lose. Expressing your truth and creativity through poem-making.* Jeremy P. Tarcher/Putman.
Fox, J. (1997). *Poetic medicine: The healing art of poem-making.* Tarcher-Putnam.
Frank, D. (Ed.). (2015). *River of earth and sky: Poems for the 21st century.* Blue Light Press.
Freeman, P. (2016). *Searching for sappho: The lost songs and world of the first woman poet.* W.W. Norton & Co.
Furman, R. (2022). *Poetry as therapy, research and education.* University Professors Press.
Garcia, L.A. (2018). *A rope of luna.* Blue Light Press.
Gasper, F. (2012). *Late rapturous.* Autumn House Press.
Gibson, A. (2021). *You better be lightning.* Button Publishing Co.
Gilbert, J. (2007). *Refusing heaven.* Knopf Publisher.
Gluck, L. (2002). *The seven ages.* Ecco Publisher.
Gluck, L. (1993). *The Wild Iris.* Ecco Publisher.
Gold, H., & Gold, A. (2024). *Father verses sons.* Rare Bird Books.
Granger, I. (2014). *The Longing in between: A poetry chaykhana anthology.* Poetry Chaikhana.
Greening, T. (2020). *Into the void: An existential psychologist faces death through poetry.* University Professors Press.
Gregg, L. (2008). *All of it singing.* Graywolf Press.
Hahn, K. (2006). *The narrow road to the interior.* W.W. Norton & Co.
Harjo, H. (2017). *Conflict resolution for holy beings.* W.W. Norton & Co.
Harjo, J. (2020). *When the light of the world was subdued, our song came through.* W.W. Norton and Co.
Hamer, M. (2023). *Spring rain.* Greystone Books.
Harrison, J. (2016, 2018). *Dead Man's Float.* Copper Canyon Press.
Harrison, J., & Kooser, T. (2003). *Braided Creek: A conversation in poetry.* Copper Canyon Press.
Hennen, T. (2013). *Darkness sticks to everything.* Copper Canyon Press.

Hess, H. (2022). Trees: *An anthology of writings and paintings* Kales Press.
Hirsch. E. (2000.) *How to read a poem and fall in love with poetry.* Ecco.
Hirschfield, J. (1997). *Nine gates: Entering the mind of poetry.* Harper Publishing.
Hirschfield, J. (2015). *Ten windows: How great poems transform the world.* Knopf Publisher.
Hoffman, L., & Moats, M. (Eds.). (2015). *Capturing shadows: Poetic encounters along the path of grief and loss.* University Professors Press.
Hoffmann, Y. (2018). *Japanese death poems: Written by Zen monks and haiku poets on the verge of death.* Tuttle.
Housden, R. (2018). *Ten poems for difficult times.* New World Library.
Howe, M. (2017). *Magdalene.* W.W. Norton & Co.
Hughes, L. (1995). *The collected poems of Langston Hughes.* Vintage Publishing.
Hynes, A. M. C., & Hynes-Berry, M. (1994). *Biblio/poetry therapy—the interactive process: A handbook.* North Star Press.
Jimenez, J. (2009) *The Poet and the sea.* (M. Berg & D. Maloney, Trans.) White Pine Press.
Kaminsky, L. (2012). *A god in the house: Poets talk about faith.* Tupelo Press.
Knill, M. & Atkins, S. (2021). *Poetry in expressive arts: Supporting resilience through poetic writing.* Jessica Kingsley Publishers.
Kooser, T. (2000). *Winter morning walks: One hundred postcards to Jim Harrison.* Carnegie Mellon Press.
Kunitz, S. (2007). *The wild braid.* W.W. Norton & Co.
Lameris, D. (2020). *Bonfire opera.* Pittsburgh Publishing.
La Tray, C. (2018). *One-sentence journal: Short poems and essays from the world at large.* Riverfeet Press.
Limon, A. (2022). *The hurting kind.* Milkweed Editions.
Loori Daido, J. (2000). *Making love with light.* Dharma Communications.
Lyon, G. E. (2021). *Back to the light.* University Press of Kentucky.
Mazza, N. (2021). *Poetry therapy: Theory and practice* (3rd ed.). Routledge.
MacFarlane, R. & Morris, J. (2020). *The lost spells.* Anansi International.
McKewen, C. (2011). *World enough and time: On Creativity and Slowing Down.* Bauhan Publishing.
McKewen, C. (2023). *In praise of listening.* Bauhan Publishing.
Mead, J. (2019). *To the wren: Collected and new poems 1991–2019.* Alice James Books.
Merwin, W. S. (1992). *The second four books of poems.* Copper Canyon Press.
Nepo, M. (2019). *Drinking from the river of light.* Soundstrue.
Norris, G. (2004). *Inviting silence.* Blueridge.

Nye, N. (2018). *Voices in the air: Poems for listeners.* Greenwillow Books.
O'Donohue, J. (2011). *Four elements: Reflections on nature.* Harmony.
Oliver, M. (2016). *Upstream: Selected essays.* Penguin Press.
Oliver, M. (2020). *Devotions: The selected poems of Mary Oliver.* Penguin Press.
Orr, G. (2002). *Poetry as survival.* The University of Georgia Press.
Phillips, T. (2017). *A humument: A treated Victorian novel.* Thames and Hudson.
Rilke, R. M. (1981). *Selected poems of Rainer Maria Rilke* (R. Bly, Trans.). Harper Perennial.
Rilke, R. M. (2000, 1929). *Letters to a young poet* (J. M. Burnham, Trans.). New World Library.
Rogers, N. (1993). *The creative connection.* Science and Behavior Books.
Rollins, A. (2019). *Library of small catastrophes.* Copper Canyon Press.
Rosen, K. (2009). *Saved by a poem: The transformative power of words.* Hay House.
Ruhl, S. (2020). *44 poems for you.* Copper Canyon Press.
Ruskin, M. (2013). *Rabindranath Tagore: Gitanjali.* Green Lotus Press.
Sardello, R. (2008). *Silence: The mystery of wholeness.* North Atlantic Books.
Sarton, M. (1995). *The house by the sea.* W.W. Norton & CO.
Schwarz, M. (2023). *When someone deeply listens to you.* River Lily Press.
Shonagon, S. (2007). *The pillow book.* Penguin Classics.
Snyder, G. (2000). *The Gary Snyder reader.* Counterpoint.
Spaulding, H. (2022). *Between us.* Alex Greene and Co.
Stafford, W. (2014). *Ask me.* Graywolf Press.
Tauma, P. (2023). *Poetry unbound.* W.W. Norton and Co.
Trommer, R. (2023). *All the honey.* Samara Press.
Wagoner, D. (1999). *Traveling light—Collected and new poems.* University of Illinois Press.
Watson, E.D. (2023). *Honey in the vein.* Bric a Brac Press.
Weingast, M. (2021). *The first free women: Original poems inspired by the early Buddhist nuns.* Shambhala.
Weller, F. (2015). *The wild edge of sorrow: Rituals of renewal and the sacred work of grief.* North Atlantic Books.
Whitman, W. (2005). *Walt Whitman's leaves of grass.* Oxford University Press.
Whyte, D. (2021). *Consolations: The solace, nourishment and underlying meaning of everyday words.* Many Rivers Press.
Wright, F. (2003). *Walking to Martha's Vineyard.* Alfred A. Knopf.
Zapruder, M. (2023). *Story of a poem.* Unnamed Press.

Media

Poetry Foundation
Poets.org
Poetry Daily
The Paris Review, "Art of Poetry" interviews
Speaking Grief https://speakinggrief.org

Poetry workshops and writing groups

Institute of Poetic Medicine
Interlochen Center for the Arts
Jackson Hole Writers
Poetry Forge
The Rowe Center

Podcasts

Commonplace. Hosted by Rachel Zucker
Interesting People Reading Poetry by Stermer Brothers
On Being. Hosted by Krista Tippet
Poetry Unbound. Hosted by Pádraig Ó Tuama.
Poetry Off the Shelf. Hosted by Helena de Groot.
The New Yorker Poetry by Kevin Young
The Poetry Exchange, Fiona Bennet and Michael Shaeffer
The Slowdown. Hosted by Major Jackson

About the Author

Terri Goslin-Jones, PhD, REACE, certified Practitioner of Poetic Medicine, unites poetic medicine with expressive arts to release inner guidance. She is a contemplative/creative and believes there is a *wise elder* within each of us that speaks in a poetic voice. Terri is co-author of *Weaving Ourselves Whole, A Guide to Forming a Transformational Expressive Arts Circle.*

She teaches graduate courses using poetry with person-centered expressive arts and serves on dissertation committees that include poetry, creativity and expressive arts-based research at Saybrook University. She also serves as consulting faculty for the PCEA program at Chinese University of Hong Kong.

Terri has designed and facilitated community poetry circles on topics such as self-compassion, death, loss, and life transition, nature/haiku, dreams, and our emotional landscape. Her creative passions include family life, expressive arts, gardening, and a love for life-long learning, physical fitness, and spirituality.

www.terrigoslin-jones.com

www.ingramcontent.com/pod-product-compliance
Lightning Source LLC
Chambersburg PA
CBHW070359240426
43671CB00013BA/2564